Breaking Through

Conversations and Prayers

Autumn Gold *Watercolour*

Eddie Askew

By the same author:

A Silence and a Shouting	*Talking with Hedgehogs*
Disguises of Love	*Unexpected Journeys*
Facing the Storm	*Love is a Wild Bird*
Breaking the Rules	*Encounters*
Cross Purposes	*Chasing the Leaves*
Slower than Butterflies	*Dabbling with Ducks*
Music on the Wind	*I've been thinking, Lord*
Edge of Daylight	*It's me again, Lord*
(Memoirs)	

Published by
TLM Trading Limited
www.tlmtrading.com

*All Bible quotations from the NEW INTERNATIONAL VERSION,
by permission of the International Bible Society.*

First published 2006, Reprinted 2012
© A.D. (Eddie) Askew, OBE © Paintings by the author

*Editorial and Design by Creative Plus Publishing Ltd.
2nd Floor, 151 High Street, Billericay, Essex, CM12 9AB
www.creative-plus.co.uk*
Printed and bound in Singapore by Imago

A catalogue record for this book is available from the British Library.
ISBN 978-0-902731-63-9

Cover picture (printed in full on pp 114-115): *Morning Flight, Watercolour*
Title page (picture printed in full on pp 106-107): *Autumn Gold, Watercolour*

Contents

Dedication

To my family, for their constant love
and encouragement.

Foreword

Eddie Askew's style of writing is such that his readers not only identify with him but, as they read, they feel understood, accepted and drawn into the felt presence of God. At least, that is what happened for me as I read the manuscript of *Breaking Through*.

One reason why I felt *understood* was because Eddie is so honest, so transparent and so real about his own experience of life and of God that it was as though he was giving *me* permission to be transparent and real too. One reason why I felt *accepted* was the unforgettable imagery that he uses as he underlines key, life-changing claims that Christians can so easily forget. Eddie recalls, for example, an occasion when, having failed God and having confessed his failure, he was not only assured that his sin had been dismissed, but he goes on to observe that God's love had been 'the first-class stamp' that sent the sin on its way. His imagery, though seemingly mundane, moves me deeply – especially as I make my almost-daily trip to the post box!

Through his powerful pen, Eddie also sets his readers free to use that much-neglected but powerful gift of God – the *imagination*. Using this gift, he transports his readers back in time and over to the place where Jesus lived and worked when he walked this earth. Gently, almost surreptitiously, Eddie encourages us so to use *our* imagination that we not only engage with but we enter into Bible passages relating to Jesus with openness and honesty – even with expectation. Eddie not only persuades us to pray in this way, he demonstrates *how* we might move in this direction. As I met the living Lord, while using some of the insights Eddie shares, time and time again my heart echoed prayers that Eddie had penned – like this one:
> 'And now, Lord of the dance, touch me
> with...healing and forgiveness and let me join you in the dance.'

As this book goes to print, my prayer is that its readers, like its author, will so *live* the Gospel stories on which the spotlight shines and so experience the ability to trust in God – even during difficult days – that they plumb more and more of the depths of the love of the God about whom Eddie feels so passionate.

Joyce Huggett
Author of *Listening to God*, published by Hodder and Stoughton.

Introduction

When I finally found the energy and courage to begin this book I'd been going through a personal rough patch. God and I hadn't been on the best of terms. Prayers seemed to go unanswered, unacknowledged, even 'returned to sender, addressee not known at this address.' I was reading the Psalms more than anything else.

I wondered if I had anything to say that might help other people. The incidents I write about almost chose themselves, as though the Lord was saying, "This is for you first and through you for others", although I'm always wary of any who claim that their words and convictions come direct from the Holy Spirit. So often, such words seem to reflect comfortably on those who make the claim; but now my prejudices are showing.

I've read these stories with imagination, lived the drama as each unfolds, scene by scene. When Galileo, the great astronomer, was called by the Inquisition to recant his observations of the way the earth moves round the sun, he said, "I do not feel obliged to believe that the same God who has endowed us with sense, reason and intellect has intended us to forgo their use." And I would add *imagination* to his list. It can draw us into an incident, make it live, and help us travel with those who shared it.

Jesus was always on the move: entering, leaving, departing, sailing. I wonder what he and his followers talked about during those long hours, days, of walking? We have only a fraction of what was said, the questions asked, the answers given, as they walked the dusty roads. I believe Jesus is still always on the move. One step ahead, and beckoning us to leave the certainties we seem rooted to, and step out into the unknown.

Eddie Askew, June 2006

Meeting under the Trees

Part One

Through the Roof

Watercolour

Reading – Mark 2:1-12

A few days later, when Jesus again entered Capernaum, the people heard that he had come home. So many gathered that there was no room left, not even outside the door, and he preached the word to them. Some men came, bringing to him a paralytic, carried by four of them. Since they could not get him to Jesus because of the crowd, they made an opening in the roof above Jesus and, after digging through it, lowered the mat the paralysed man was lying on. When Jesus saw their faith, he said to the paralytic, "Son, your sins are forgiven."

Now some teachers of the law were sitting there, thinking to themselves, "Why does this fellow talk like that? He's blaspheming! Who can forgive sins but God alone?"

Immediately Jesus knew in his spirit that this was what they were thinking in their hearts, and he said to them, "Why are you thinking these things? Which is easier: to say to the paralytic, 'Your sins are forgiven,' or to say, 'Get up, take your mat and walk'? But that you may know that the Son of Man has authority on earth to forgive sins..." He said to the paralytic, "I tell you, get up, take your mat and go home." He got up, took his mat and walked out in full view of them all. This amazed everyone and they praised God, saying, "We have never seen anything like this!"

Imagine...

The first small specks of dust falling on the immaculately clean clothes of the Pharisees alert them. The small specks become bigger, adding to their annoyance as they try to brush them off. Then there's a scraping noise, and small cracks appear in the mud plaster between the roof timbers. Everyone in the crowded room looks up. Even Jesus, as he pauses in his talk. A murmur goes round the room.

It's crowded. In front, some Pharisees – the 'separated ones' – who obey every facet of Jewish law and set themselves up as role models for the rest of the community. Some of the law teachers too, the Scribes, who study, expand and interpret the law into great complexity. They've come from all over Galilee and beyond to see and hear Jesus. Behind them, pressing up close, ordinary folk. Men only, of course; women aren't allowed in. The people of Capernaum, fishermen and farmers, carpenters and boat builders, shopkeepers who'd thought this meeting important enough to close down for the afternoon. They're particularly interested in Jesus because he's local. Living in the town, temporarily at least, here in Peter's home. Every space is filled, not even elbow room left, with others standing around the walls, unable to find floor space to sit. The room is hot and getting hotter. Sweat runs down their faces and necks, wets their robes. No breath of air – until the hole in the roof gets bigger.

They've all been listening quietly to Jesus; some with rapt attention, others puzzled, the Pharisees frowning, wondering how to react to this new teacher with a growing reputation as a healer. Until the dust starts to fall. Then a small hole appears, wide enough for a weather-beaten hand to push through and begin to break off bigger pieces of plaster. The hole widens, a head peers down but quickly withdraws. The murmuring gets louder, there's a last fall of debris, and the hole is wide enough. A mat appears, catches on the rough edges of the hole, and is pushed through. As it's lowered, they see a man, all skin and bones. He can't weigh very much or the mat wouldn't have held him. He's balanced precariously and, with what little strength he has, he holds on and shouts, eyes wide in panic. No-one moves to help. They can't move, they're all too surprised and packed in too tightly.

Then Peter gets up, struggles through the crowd with difficulty and reaches the outside steps to the roof. Halfway up he stops; the men have already lowered their burden through the hole. He's too late, and there are at least four of them. He turns round and forces his way back inside.

The man bumps to the ground in front of Jesus. His mat, even his arms and legs, are lying across the feet of the listeners. Immediately the pandemonium lessens, and is replaced by muttered questions. "What's happening?" "Who's the man?" Folk look at Jesus. How will he react? Will he be annoyed at the interruption to the flow of his teaching, or exasperated by yet another demand on his time and energy? The man on the mat is bewildered, embarrassed. He doesn't know what to do. There's not much he can do, in his condition. He hasn't engineered this, and he's angry at the over-enthusiasm of the four idiots who've dragged him here. It's all their fault. He'd rather be at home than at the centre of a scene like this, especially seeing the Pharisees within arm's length. He doesn't want to take the blame. He begins to apologise.

To those sitting close to Jesus, there seems to be the shadow of a smile on his face, even the suspicion of a grin round the corners of his mouth. Perhaps the unorthodox approach of breaking through the roof appeals to his sense of humour. The man's whole attention is suddenly drawn to Jesus' face. Their eyes meet. For a moment there's no sound, then Jesus speaks.

A few days later, when Jesus again entered Capernaum,
the people heard that he had come home.
So many gathered that there was no room left,
not even outside the door, and he preached the word to them.

Mark 2:1-2

It's great to come home. My work took me all over the world, often into
poor and still-developing countries, where travel and living conditions
were rough. I was away for a month, six weeks at a time, and my family
were very forgiving. Travel was fascinating, but tiring, and it was always
good to get home, to people I knew and loved, and who loved me.
Capernaum wasn't Jesus' family home. That was in Nazareth, but there
were tensions at times with his own human family. So, once he'd begun
gathering followers around him and gone public, Capernaum became his
second home. Specifically it was his disciple Peter's home.

As time went on there were other homes, like that of Mary, Martha, and
Lazarus in Bethany. (Luke 10:38) Places where Jesus could shelter from
the pressures, which were mounting up, and find the loving care and
peace he needed. But there was no peace and quiet in Peter's home this
time. Modern excavation has uncovered a site in Capernaum with early
Christian inscriptions, which strongly identify it as Peter's home. It was
only a short distance from the synagogue, and was within the town.
A crowd could gather quickly. This one did. The guest room filled first.
A few of the elite turned up – Scribes and Pharisees expecting respect,
taking the best places, sitting on the mats and commandeering the
cushions. They were here for a purpose. It was two or three days' journey
from Jerusalem, but they'd thought it important enough to come to hear
this new teacher with his forthright opinions. Behind them sat ordinary
townsmen. Then others crowding round the door, on tiptoe to see, spilling
out into the courtyard and beyond the gate into the road.

'And he preached to them.' Sorry, but I don't think so. Not in the way
most preachers preach today. In my imagination I see and hear it as a
question and answer session. Jesus listening courteously and closely to the
concerns people had. Then helping them towards a clearer understanding
of how God yearned for them to live. But he senses a divided crowd. Some
taking his teaching to heart, gladly and with wonder – "Why have I never
seen it that way before?" Others beginning to bristle. Jesus sees them
stiffen, the tension in their bodies growing. Before the day ends they must
be challenged. And here's an opportunity both to heal the man – Jesus'
priority – and use the opportunity to discomfort those who opposed him.

Lord, it's sometimes hard
to accept the new.
Not when I've thought of it, of course,
and cannot understand why others
are so slow to see it clear –
but when the new slips sideways,
unannounced, into my life,
challenging change,
upsetting all the assumptions
on which I base my thoughts.
Then, I dig ditches, raise my defences,
refuse to negotiate.

Oh I pretend all right,
let others think I'm open to the new,
but lurking in the background all unseen
another programme runs,
blocking unwelcome truths I do not want to hear.
I'd rather trundle down the ruts I've made,
well-worn and getting deeper every day.
No need to change.
Easy to settle on second-best,
or third, but let's not look at that.

So, Lord, I know the score.
I turn your living word to stone,
and keep it, petrified,
a sad memorial
to all the eagerness to learn
I used to show.
Please wake me, shake me up,
surprise and startle me to life.
Open my eyes, my heart and mind
until I see again
the beauty of your presence
and your truth.

Some men came, bringing to him a paralytic,
carried by four of them.

Mark 2:3

The writer, Albert Camus, said that friends don't walk in front of you, or behind you, they walk alongside you. The men certainly did that as they took turns carrying the paralysed man. We don't know how or when he became paralysed. It could have been a sudden illness, a stroke maybe, or an accident; falling awkwardly from an olive tree, or slipping off a ladder while repairing his home. It might even have been falling off or even through a roof! That could have given his friends the idea for what they did. Whatever it was, he'd made friends who were there for him when he needed them. It suggests too, that he'd been a good friend to them in happier days, because they wouldn't have done for a stranger what they did for him. True friendships, the sort that make people willing to give up a whole day to carry him to Jesus in such an unconventional way, take time to grow.

Mark's Gospel doesn't call them friends, just men. Luke's account is the same. They might have been hired hands, but I don't think so. Hired hands could have carried the man to Jesus, but they wouldn't have had the nerve to heft him up the outside staircase, and risk the wrath of the house owner by breaking into his roof. Only very good friends would have done that. Hired hands would have seen the crowd, made a feeble attempt to get through, and then given up. "It's no use. We can't get through. You'd better come back another day." They would have left the decision to him. His bearers went way beyond this. I'm sure they were his friends.

I see them trying hard to push through the crowd. "Please, let us through, we must get in. We've got a sick man here." It's no use, however persistent they are. There were other sick people in the throng, all equally desperate. Everyone wanted to get to Jesus. "What makes you so special?" they ask. And there were sharp elbows and sharper tongues resisting them. Angry comments hissed from inside the courtyard for quiet. But the friends react. "If you think we've brought him all this way for nothing you're wrong. We're not going back now."

However, they do pull back, just for a moment. They set the stretcher down, look at each other, and wipe the sweat away. With increasing frustration, one of the men – a lateral thinker – suggests the unthinkable. "Come on," he says, "through the roof." The others are astonished. One frowns, another raises his eyebrows, but a third grins and answers, "Let's give it a go." And before they realise what they're doing, and not listening to their sick friend's protests, they grab the corners of the mat. In a moment, they're up above the crowd and working out exactly where they should break through. Thank God for true friends.

I thank you, Lord,
that I have never had to break a hole
through any roof to get to you.
There was a time
when crowding questions
kept me from your door.
Times when I struggled,
wondered what I had to do or be –
not realising I only had to be myself –
to get to you.
And then that glorious moment
when I turned,
and knew that you were there beside me.
Closer than thought.
No roof, no walls, no crowd
could ever get between.
Yet there are times, Lord,
when I can't feel you near
as once you were,
when life gets tough
and I am walking on my own,
or seem to be.
But I walk on in faith –
accompanied occasionally by an angry shout,
which you don't seem to mind –
trusting that you're still there.
And though I cannot see or feel you close,
I know from past experience
that at a time you choose –
your time, not mine –
you'll show yourself again,
and I will hear you say
"I told you so."
I'll hang on, Lord,
it seems to be the only thing to do.

I thank you, Lord,
that I have never had to break a hole
through any roof to get to you.

Striking a Bargain, Kathmandu, Nepal

Watercolour

Since they could not get him to Jesus because of the crowd,
they made an opening in the roof above Jesus and, after digging
through it, lowered the mat the paralysed man was lying on.

Mark 2:4

In these stories, we rarely get to see inside the sufferer's mind. He's given no name and there's no "this is how he felt." The writer concentrates on the basics: "This man was sick, Jesus healed him." End of story. But I always want to know more. I try to imagine his fear and frustration. The potions and pills, herbs and prayers, had left him as he was, no better and deeply depressed. He's angry at his helplessness, his moods swing, and always there are the questions. "Why me? What have I done to deserve this?" Theology gives us answers of a sort, but it doesn't take away the questions. Not for me, anyway. How long had the man been helpless, how deeply did he long to be well and active again? How often had he endured the well-meaning platitudes of friends, when he would rather they had sat by him in silent sympathy? Maybe he'd given up; reached a point of resignation or bleak despair, and was living now without any hope for the future. Until Jesus came.

What of his family? Their worries, their financial problems, their inability to do much to help; other than stand by him in their common sadness and hurt. Was it his family or friends who'd heard that Jesus was home in Capernaum and suggested that they take him there? Did he want to go, or would he rather have stayed at home? He'd had his hopes raised many times. And all for nothing. Whatever it was, by the time his friends had clashed with the crowd and got him halfway up the outside staircase, it was all out of his control. All he could do, assuming his hands still had some strength in them, was to hold onto the edges of his mat and pray that he wouldn't fall off.

The first thing Jesus and his audience knew was the scraping noise. Then dust falling on them, its specks bright and golden in a shaft of sunlight from the open window. The picture is almost one from a Monty Python sketch. A hole in the roof and a bearded face peering down, trying to decide which of the upturned faces was Jesus.

I wonder how much teaching he was able to give with so many interruptions, but the way he dealt with them was a core part of his teaching anyway. I use the Internet a lot. I keyed in the word 'interruptions'. Hundreds of hits came up and all the relevant ones, without exception, talked about ways of avoiding them. Interruptions are seen as time-wasters, a nuisance. Jesus saw them as opportunities: to heal and encourage the sick and anxious, to develop relationships, to illustrate his teaching. Above all, interruptions offered him the chance to talk about God's kingdom, the community of believers. I wish I could see interruptions like that when I'm struggling with my writing and a friend phones just to chat. But now, one more interruption and the sick man is face to face with Jesus.

Lord, it's all the interruptions.
I just can't count the times
I've asked for patience,
and still you don't respond.
Patience to deal with all the folk
who punctuate my time with calls.
The phone at home is bad enough,
but now I am supposed
to carry one around with me all day –
mobile they call it,
and I wonder
would you have switched it off
if you'd had one?
I like the name they use in other places –
cell-phone.
That says it clear. It locks me in,
boxes me,
at everybody's call.

There, now I've got that off my chest
I'm coming back to patience
and my lack of it.
It's hard enough to organise
the things I have to do
without all these distractions.

A little space to think, Lord,
that's what I need.
And then I could walk quietly through my world,
at ease, enjoying every moment
and, so courteously,
with greater understanding,
welcome those I choose to recognise.
A gracious listener,
spreading hope along the path.
But what you seem to give
is just the opposite.
You mark my time
with challenges along the way,
with folk who need more time and energy
than I'm inclined to give.

You abrade my day with roughness
but when I find my voice
and register my protest,
I hear a still small voice that says
that serving them is serving you.
It doesn't make it easier, Lord,
but maybe just a little more acceptable.

Morning at the Temple

Forgiven, Lord,
and just like that?
I know it's true,
although it's unbelievable
in any other context but your love.

A. D. ASKEW

Watercolour

> When Jesus saw their faith, he said to the paralytic,
> "Son, your sins are forgiven."
>
> Mark 2:5

There he was, lying on his mat on the floor, alone in the crowded room. His friends were still on the roof, peering down through the hole they'd made. The house still surrounded by a multitude who, minutes earlier, had refused to let them pass. Now they were expecting an argument about damage to the roof. Happily, the outcome was more positive. As the man was lowered down, the front row of listeners, Pharisees and Scribes, tried to move away, not wanting the man to land on them. But space was limited, and however much they shuffled back, they'd still have a pretty close encounter with what happened next.

After his initial surprise, Jesus reacts calmly. He doesn't ask what the man or his friends want, that was obvious. Equally obvious was their faith. They'd gone to a lot of trouble to get him to Jesus. Risked the anger of the house owner, and the annoyance of the crowd at the interruption. The men certainly had faith although the story says nothing about the sick man's faith. He was too busy hanging on to his mat, too embarrassed and apprehensive to say or ask for anything. But his friends' faith was enough. I reckon that's true today when we pray for our friends. It may be what we do for them, rather than what they are able to do for themselves, that really counts.

It does leave me wondering though, about how the pious Pharisees now thought of Jesus, already established as a healer. If, as they believed, illness came from God as a result of sin, then anyone with the power to heal must be in a special relationship with God. Jesus' next words confirm this. "Son," he says, "your sins are forgiven." Tom Wright, theologian and writer, tells us that the original word translated as forgiven, literally means 'sent away' or 'dismissed'. "Your sin is sent away. God isn't angry with you. You can be whole again." * God's love and healing power pour through Jesus. And in calling him "Son" Jesus draws him into a family relationship with himself and, through him, with God the Father.

* *From* Matthew for Everyone *by Tom Wright, SPCK 2002*

Faith can break through the roof of the possible and push the boundaries of what we believe and what we can do. Faith took Jesus and his followers into danger and conflict. Faith tells us, sometimes even appears to compel us, to attempt the impossible. For the man, wholeness was just a step away. He couldn't take that step, but Jesus could.

Forgiven, Lord,
and just like that?
I know it's true,
although it's unbelievable
in any other context than your love.
I sometimes feel for all I've done
or not done when I ought,
there should be something still
that marks me out a sinner.
A suspended sentence at the very least.
But no, it's gone,
my sin dismissed,
your love the first-class stamp
that sends it on its way.
I'm breathless when I think of it.

And here I am,
clutching the mat of hope on which I lie.
The only certainty I have –
suspended in mid air,
between the ropes of doubt and faith –
is that you are down there waiting.
Not high in clouds,
mist-hidden, nebulous,
where I can't reach,
but in my world,
ground level zero.
Offering the strength
to stand and face the world
with all its obstacles
and start again.
Not on my own
but, glory be, with you.

Now some teachers of the law were sitting there, thinking to themselves," Why does this fellow talk like that? He's blaspheming! Who can forgive sins but God alone?"

Mark 2:6-7

Jesus doesn't simply heal. Actually, he delayed the physical healing for a few moments to look at the spiritual leaders sitting in front of him, their lives made sterile by their rules. Minds set hard in the concrete of legalism, with little love and no joy. He takes a deep breath, and deliberately creates a major confrontation. He says the most provocative words he could say, to such an influential group of people.

It was an important occasion for them. They'd come "from every village of Galilee and from Judea and Jerusalem." (Luke 5:17) An indication of their alarm. They'd gathered to see and hear for themselves what this new teacher had to say. He was causing anxiety, even in Jerusalem. The Pharisees were a sort of Orwellian 'thought police', intent on preserving the purity of their religion. Some, no doubt, came to listen sincerely. Others came with their prejudice already sharpened, waiting to pounce on the least irregularity in what Jesus said.

His words shocked them to the core. They believed it was only by observing scrupulously every single nuance of the Jewish law that they could please God. But suddenly Jesus appeared from nowhere offering unconditional love. A challenge to the Pharisees' influence over the people.

The atmosphere in the room changes as Jesus speaks. There's a sudden chill in the air. No-one moves, but shoulders tense, mouths tighten, frowns deepen. Jesus reads their body language, their thoughts clear to him in their shocked and angry expressions. "He's talking as though he were God himself," they think. They were right of course: only God can forgive sin. The problem was the gap between what they believed and who Jesus was. On each side of the chasm between Jesus and the Pharisees, the desire was the same – to find forgiveness and acceptance – but the 'how' was different. For the Pharisees the only way was a lifetime of rule keeping. Jesus invites them to a dramatic and immediate leap of faith across the divide into the arms of a loving and forgiving God. Thomas Merton, 20th Century monk and mystic wrote, "Our sinful self is not our true self." Jesus was offering them the opportunity to rediscover who they truly were, and to regain their identity as children of God, but that was too much for them.

And now,
Lord of the dance,
touch me
with that same healing and
forgiveness,
and let me join you in the dance.

St Niklaus Church, Prague

Watercolour

Lord, living by the rules
seems so much easier.
To know just how and where I'm going
and mark behaviour out of ten,
occasional gold stars stuck in the margin.

But rules make other rules,
one on another,
and soon there'd be a towering edifice
of do's and don'ts
to govern every hour of my life.
But mostly don'ts.
My pathway blocked by guilt,
my failures hard and cold,
and I would lose
what little virtue I had thought to hold.

But as I shiver in the winter of my weakness,
your invitation loves me into life.
Just one way out,
the easiest and the hardest.
To give my pride a push –
although there's little of it left by now –
and open up my life to your forgiveness.
That way lies freedom.
Lord, just let me get my breath.

..and he said to them, "Why are you thinking these things? Which is easier: to say to the paralytic, 'Your sins are forgiven,' or to say, 'Get up, take your mat and walk'? But that you may know that the Son of Man has authority on earth to forgive sins..." He said to the paralytic, "I tell you, get up, take your mat and go home." He got up, took his mat and walked out in full view of them all. This amazed everyone and they praised God, saying, "We have never seen anything like this!"

Mark 2: 8-12

Jesus looks his critics in the eye, going from one to the next, and I doubt if any could hold the challenge of his gaze for long. He's agreeing with them. Only the power of God can cure illness, he says, just as only God can forgive sins. And in giving the man strength to walk, Jesus links the two together. The most astounding claim he could make: that the power of God was at work through him. "If I can heal, as I am about to do," he says, "there's only one possible conclusion – that I can also offer God's forgiveness." A conclusion it's impossible for them to take in.

He strengthens his challenge and shocks them even more by his use of the title 'Son of Man'. In Jewish belief, Son of Man was the name of the one to whom God would give both glory and authority at the final judgement, when God's rule would be fully established on earth. In other words, it meant the Messiah. And while they were reeling from the shock of this claim, Jesus piles on the pressure.

He turns to the man on the mat, whose sudden appearance had changed an intense but quiet discussion of his teaching into a sensational confrontation. He must have been bewildered by the heated exchanges going on above his head – it was above his head in every sense, as he lay on the floor. Jesus turns back to him. "Get up," says Jesus, holding the man's gaze intently, "pick your mat up, and go home." No ritual, no strange ceremony, just simple words. I see the man as he stands, so excited that his arm gets tangled in one of the ropes used to lower him through the roof. "Immediately" says Luke 5:25. I love all the immediates scattered through these reports. No long wait to see the medical consultant, no repeat visits to the physiotherapist, effective and helpful as these can be. Perhaps the man's a little rocky on his feet as he takes his first tentative steps. Then a gasp, from him and the audience, and a look of developing confidence on his face. His arms go out to gain balance. He stoops to pick up his mat, nearly overbalances but not quite, and begins to walk through the crowd. There's no need for him to push; even in the crowded room people seem to find the space to let him through A few reach out to touch him. The argument means little to him. He has been touched by love, and he can walk. Nothing else matters.

His friends rush down the staircase, shouting a welcome. "We knew it would work. We knew he could." As they walk home together, they keep their eyes on him, all still excited and full of wonder. They offer their arms on the rough patches of the road but he refuses.

With each step he grows stronger, his confidence increasing. One friend tries to take his mat but he smiles and holds on to it. I suspect he kept it near him in the days to come, a treasured reminder of what Jesus had done. Something he would point to often as he grew old and repeated the story yet again to a long-suffering family.

I guess there would still be hard times for him in the years ahead, but the memory and reality of his healing would give him the strength to face the world. The audience left behind in Peter's home was amazed and praised God. Except the Pharisees and teachers of the law. They were still shaken by the claims Jesus had made, and the power he'd shown to back up the claims. They had much to think about. Later, when Peter was grumbling into his beard about the damage to his roof, I think Jesus must have said, "It's a small price to pay, Peter, for a man's healing."

Just walked, Lord?
I can go along with that
for his first few steps
before he gained a little confidence
and, more important, trusted you
and what you'd done for him.
But on the way back home?
Just walking, Lord?
Not dancing?

I think he was.
Arms out, head high,
feet dancing to a rhythm
he had never known before.
Maybe his friends danced too,
although they'd had the strain
of carrying him one way.

Dancing his freedom.
Freed from his mat, his bed at home,
freed from the helplessness
that made him victim.

Dancing his pain away,
pain that lay with him night and day,
an intimate companion
who'd far outstayed its welcome.

Dancing away his anger and his shame.
Anger with God at his condition,
the shame and deep-felt unnamed guilt,
unspoken but as real as pain,
and part of it.

Dancing his joy
at sin sent far away,
forgiven and forgotten,
life renewed.

Dancing into an unknown future,
but confident
that you dance with him
and he'd never dance alone.

And now,
Lord of the dance,
touch me
with that same healing and forgiveness,
and let me join you in the dance.

Saint Mark's Square, Venice

Part Two

Wider Horizons

Watercolour

Reading – Luke 7:1-10

When Jesus had finished saying all this in the hearing of the people, he entered Capernaum.

There a centurion's servant, whom his master valued highly, was sick and about to die. The centurion heard of Jesus and sent some elders of the Jews to him, asking him to come and heal his servant. When they came to Jesus, they pleaded earnestly with him, "This man deserves to have you do this, because he loves our nation and has built our synagogue." So Jesus went with them.

He was not far from the house when the centurion sent friends to say to him: "Lord, don't trouble yourself, for I do not deserve to have you come under my roof. That is why I did not even consider myself worthy to come to you. But say the word, and my servant will be healed. For I myself am a man under authority, with soldiers under me. I tell this one, 'Go,' and he goes; and that one, 'Come', and he comes. I say to my servant, 'Do this', and he does it."

When Jesus heard this, he was amazed at him, and turning to the crowd following him, he said, "I tell you, I have not found such great faith even in Israel." Then the men who had been sent returned to the house and found the servant well.

Reading – Matthew 8:5-13

When Jesus had entered Capernaum, a centurion came to him, asking for help. "Lord," he said, "my servant lies at home paralysed and in terrible suffering." Jesus said to him, "I will go and heal him."

The centurion replied, "Lord, I do not deserve to have you come under my roof. But just say the word, and my servant will be healed. For I myself am a man under authority, with soldiers under me. I tell this one, 'Go,' and he goes; and that one, 'Come,' and he comes. I say to my servant 'Do this,' and he does it."

When Jesus heard this, he was astonished and said to those following him, "I tell you the truth, I have not found anyone in Israel with such great faith. I say to you that many will come from the east and the west, and will take their places at the feast with Abraham, Isaac and Jacob in the kingdom of heaven. But the subjects of the kingdom will be thrown outside, into the darkness, where there will be weeping and gnashing of teeth."

Then Jesus said to the centurion, "Go! It will be done just as you believed it would." And his servant was healed at that very hour.

Imagine...

I guess great Caesar in Rome had never heard of Capernaum. Just a small town on the edge of a not-very-big lake in a remote province of a widespread empire. But Capernaum is always busy. It's a fishing village on the edge of Galilee, and also a trade centre. Two important highways cross here. One from Damascus to Caesaria Maritima on the Mediterranean coast; the other from the great port of Tyre to Egypt. Capernaum is a Jewish village, but folk of many nationalities pass through, mostly traders. That's why a Roman centurion with his troops is stationed here. There's also an official tax collector named Levi who would soon be invited to follow Jesus.

Today, there's more activity than usual, and a feeling of anticipation. Jesus has been out on the road again but is coming back. The news has arrived first, and people are expecting him. They stand at the roadside, blocking access to the shops and stalls, and tripping over the ubiquitous beggars. Others squat in little groups, talking, laughing, marvelling at the news of another healing miracle Jesus had worked, and trying to unfold the meaning of the stories he'd told. And, of course, anyone who's beginning to annoy the authorities is popular with ordinary folk.

It's a warm day, only a little breeze ruffles the palm trees, hardly enough to cool the crowd. The shops fill the air with the scent of spices, sweet and heady. Stronger smells too. The pungent odour of fish drying on the beach nearby. The smell of pack horses, donkeys, camels and the dust they kick up. The unmistakable scent of a close press of people. More gather; it's getting difficult to push through.

Now, in the distance, there's a group of people walking this way. They seem light-hearted, and give us the feeling that it's good to be alive. They don't carry much – just a few bundles of clothing slung over their shoulders, and their walking sticks to lever them up the hillsides. Their robes are hitched up above their knees, their legs and feet the colour of the dusty road. Around and behind them others walk, looking, listening, occasionally shouting a question. Their attention focuses on one man in the middle. It's Jesus.

Then, from the town, another little band of people appears. They walk more slowly, sedately, their beards and clothing well groomed. Jewish elders. The two groups meet and pause. The disciples a little wary, the elders not quite sure how to address this new and unorthodox teacher.

Some of them had been in the synagogue when Jesus had been there, and seen a demonstration of his power. Now, they want to ask a favour. Jesus stands with a welcoming but slightly quizzical smile on his face. He waits, his eyes moving from one face to another. The crowd surrounds them, and the elders look to their spokesman. He edges nearer, leans forward, wishing the interview could have been more private, coughs to clear his throat, and begins.

"We have a friend," he says and pauses, looking slightly apologetic. "Actually he's a Roman, a centurion. No, wait, he really is a friend, even though he's a Gentile. He's very sympathetic. He built our new synagogue. You've been there, taught there." He's almost gabbling with embarrassment by now, but Jesus listens courteously. "His servant is sick, he believes you can heal him. Please will you go, he deserves your help?" Hearing him, some in the crowd grin at the elders' discomfort. Others look surprised to hear an elder saying something good about Romans. They're the enemy, the occupiers. Surely Jesus won't go with them to help a Roman? And who's this coming down the road? It's him, the centurion himself.

There, a centurion's servant, whom his master valued highly,
was sick and about to die. The centurion heard of Jesus
and sent some of the elders of the Jews to him,
asking him to come and heal his servant.

Luke 7:2-3

The healing of the paralysed man began with surprise – not many patients enter hospital through the roof – and ended in discord, with the Pharisees shocked and angry. This event starts more positively, but with some unusual relationships. There's the Roman centurion's unexpected care for his servant; then Jewish elders are seen supporting the centurion himself. And it ends with Jesus welcoming into the kingdom, not only a Roman officer, but all who have faith in him, whatever their background.

Jesus has finished a long day's teaching in the hills behind the town. A tiring day, answering people's questions, projecting his voice so that all could hear, and then a dusty walk back, fortunately down hill. He must have been hoping for a rest, a break in the demands, but he's met by yet another cry for help.

There is, though, one dark note. Let's not blur the picture; the servant is a slave. Rome was built on the work of slaves. They had no human rights, something the centurion accepts without question as part of his culture. But the slave was a valuable piece of property, and it was as important to keep him healthy as it was to care for your horse. But is that all?

There's something more to this than the centurion simply protecting his own interests. Listen to his words, according to Matthew. "Lord," he says, "my servant lies at home paralysed" – a cool statement of fact – "and in terrible suffering." In those last words, the centurion recognises the man's pain; shows real compassion and concern for him. It's a deeper feeling than that usually found between master and slave. Doctor Luke adds "and about to die," stressing the urgency. The centurion compromises himself in seeking Jesus' help, but he's ready to go to any lengths to get his slave well, even asking the help of one whom he might have seen as a troublemaker, one to keep his official eye on.

He'd heard of Jesus, of course. It was his job to keep the area policed, patrolled, and trouble free. He'd also built up a rapport with Capernaum's Jewish inhabitants and, whether he attended the synagogue or not, he was credited with building it. As a 'God-fearer' – if that's what he was, a Gentile who worshipped with the Jews and recognised the one, true God

– he would have heard them talking about Jesus, and wondering at his healing powers. I guess too, that the centurion had already called in local doctors to treat his servant, without success. Now he breaks through racial, political, social and religious boundaries to help his slave.

I wonder too, if the centurion's use of the word *home* rang a bell with Jesus? (Matthew 8:6) Capernaum had become home for both of them, in each case by adoption. Jesus because it was a good centre for his work throughout Galilee, the centurion because he was sent there.

Jesus responds, reaching across those same boundaries. Just as suffering recognises no barriers, so compassion ignores them. I ask too whether Jesus felt a special sympathy for the slave because that's how Jesus was later to describe himself. He told his inner, more intimate group of followers, "...Whoever wants to be great among you must be your servant, and whoever wants to be first must be your slave – just as the Son of Man did not come to be served, but to serve and to give his life as a ransom for many." (Matthew 20:26-28) Ransom, of course, being the price paid to free a slave, and freedom was what Jesus was offering. And, in Jesus the two things combine uniquely: authority and service.

You must have thought of home, Lord,
many times.
And so must he, the centurion.
I don't know where he'd once called home,
the family he'd been a part of,
or how he'd felt on leaving it.
Was it adventure,
young man's rebellion,
or was he dragged unwillingly to war?
Whatever way,
I'm sure his thoughts went home
from time to time,
helped maybe in an evening
with a cup of local red.
Or two.
Longing for old familiar landscapes
painted on his mind,
in colours faded over time.
Ready for peace and rest,
for home.

You understood, I'm sure.
You were an exile too,
an exile in the world you'd helped create.
And some days in your morning prayers,
alone up on the mountain side,
I'm sure you yearned for home.
That place of love and joy
you'd left behind to bring a soldier home,
the centurion, one whose faith and trust
outshone the rest.
And others too, like me,
who cannot claim
the strength of faith he showed,
but this I know –
that as you welcomed him with joy
you welcome all
who find the faith to ask your help.

And now, Lord,
let me ask just one small thing –
that one day I may meet him
to exchange experience,
and tell him how his story
sparked my imagination,
strengthened my faith.

That breaking through
the fences of my fears
I find new freedom
to explore a universe of love.
Expanding universe.
The further I explore
the wider its horizons grow.

A. D. ASKEW

Where Sea Meets Sky

Watercolour

> When they came to Jesus, they pleaded earnestly with him,
> "This man deserves to have you do this, because he loves
> our nation and has built our synagogue.
>
> Luke 7:4-5

Jesus and the elders must have met before. He'd preached in the Capernaum synagogue, and had healed a man possessed by an evil spirit. (Luke 4: 31-37) It's not easy to sort out how the elders felt. Uneasy, I'm sure. Eyebrows must have been raised as they spoke so warmly to Jesus on behalf of a Roman officer and his slave, both foreigners and Gentiles. They were perhaps reluctant too, to be seen so sympathetic to the local representative of the occupying power. They were conscious of all the help he'd given them, but they were hesitant to ask this controversial new teacher for help, even if he had made Capernaum his home. Usually, they were in a position of influence, but now they are the supplicants.

They make the best of it, and give the centurion a great end-of-term report. "He loves our nation," they said. Most Romans saw them as a proud, unruly, uncompromising and unmanageable nation of troublemakers. Somehow, the centurion had gone beyond this and had found their faith attractive. Perhaps, as a man with an enquiring mind and broad sympathies, his time in Capernaum had given him space to think.

Then the elders make an astonishing assertion. "He built our synagogue." Why had they not built their own synagogue? Centurions, junior officers, were not wealthy men. Where did he find the money? Did he encourage his legionaries to dig the foundations? Perhaps he'd used his influence in fund-raising, persuading others to part with their cash. I doubt if sponsored walks were on the agenda in those days, although in another context Jesus did look at the Roman practice of forced labour, and recommended that if someone makes you go one mile, you should go with him for two. (Matthew 5:41)

The truth is we don't know the detail, although I for one would love to find out. I suppose the important thing is that the Lord knows and that's enough.

Space to think, Lord,
that's what I need.
The time to face in quiet
some of the challenges
you put to me.
And courage too,
to help break through
the inhibitions and the fears
that hold me back,
set boundaries and fence me in.
They come, so often, camouflaged,
disguised in comfort,
whispering that this way
life is easier,
the journey smoother,
and there'll be companions on the road.

But something deep inside,
your voice, I think –
so nearly overlaid by other sounds
but never quite drowned out –
tells me there's more to life than this.
That breaking through the fences of my fears
I find new freedom to explore a universe of love.
Expanding universe.
The further I explore
the wider its horizons grow.
The more I take the more there is,
and with your help I'm free to love myself
and those I never thought to love.

> When Jesus had entered Capernaum, a centurion came to him,
> asking for help. "Lord," he said, "my servant lies at home
> paralysed and in terrible suffering."
>
> Matthew 8:5-6

We have two versions of this story, one told by Matthew, the other by
Luke. They differ in some details. Not surprising really. Eye-witnesses
remember differently, and when their accounts are passed on by word of
mouth over the years, facts get modified before ever they are written
down. Luke tells us that the centurion first sends Jewish elders, then sends
friends, but Matthew says the Roman came himself. Perhaps both are
true: that the centurion sent the elders to prepare the ground by speaking
first, and then his friends before he arrives himself. Good tactics from a
commander of soldiers to send an advance guard to secure the ground.

My imagination sees the two meeting, the centurion and Jesus. Both men
with authority, both in control of the destinies of the people under their
care. Jesus is in his travel-worn and not-so-clean robe, dusty from the
road, the other smartly dressed, as a Roman officer would be. He's
mature, stocky, scarred, his hair clipped short, clean shaven and fit. He
knows how to handle people, both soldiers and civilians. He walks with
confidence, but he's a little in awe of Jesus. This is the first time he's met a
prophet, a God-man, face to face. He's not quite sure how Jesus will react.
He knows he mustn't touch Jesus, contact with a Gentile would make
Jesus unclean. Maybe he should treat him like a senior officer, cool and
respectful? But underlying his correctness is real concern for his suffering
slave. Jesus looks at him. He reads his body language, and smiles a
welcome to put him more at ease. And waits.

The elders have taken a quiet step back. Now the Roman must speak for
himself. The conversation is brief and to the point. Soldiers don't waste
words. "My servant is sick and in agony. Will you please help?" If Jesus
was surprised, he hid it well. He asks no questions. No challenging, "Why
do you, a Roman, ask me for help?" Jesus recognises the centurion's
sincerity and concern for his slave. Jesus and the soldier step out together.
The disciples follow, eyebrows raised, but quiet. They are beginning to
realise that they can never predict how Jesus will react to a new situation,
except that he will always respond to human need.

Jesus still surprises. Something that makes me cautious when I hear the
claims of some evangelists and church leaders. Those who preach their
own version of the gospel with a burning conviction of their own

righteousness, and who lay out a detailed pattern of lifestyle for their followers, claiming aggressively that their way is the only way to follow Jesus. It seems not far from the rigid stance the Pharisees took. And if Jesus could amaze the Pharisees with how he behaved, he can still amaze us today.

You offer love without reserve.
No rules apply,
and no small print...

Blue Winter

Watercolour

Lord, when I'm not sure
just where to turn
or what to do,
do I detect a smile?
I see you like the Cheshire cat –
forgive the simile, no disrespect intended –
who slowly disappeared in front of Alice,
leaving nothing but its smile.
Until, in turn, that disappeared
and she was left alone.
It's just that I'm not always sure
how you would act in certain situations,
nor what you'd want of me.

I only know
that when I'm at my most dogmatic,
a niggling question mark
dances before my eyes
and asks me if I'm really sure
that's what you'd do.
But this I know for sure,
or think I do –
now guard me from quick judgement –
that you'd be ruled by love
and love is ruled by nothing but itself.
A love that breaks through human boundaries
in face of need.
Lord, keep me ever sensitive to that,
and those who need my love.

Questioning looks, eyes raised. "Just say the word," says the centurion.
He believes. It's the quiet, firm voice of the soldier. I don't hear it as a
reasoned statement, not something he's thought about, a conclusion
reached after weighing all the facts. I hear it as a sudden conviction, the
sort of decision a commander may have to make in an emergency, a rush
of certainty formed as he stands before Jesus. A dramatic conversion.
Jesus asks nothing about the sick slave. All that matters is that he's ill, in
agony and near death, and that another man cares for him, with the faith
to open up his life to Jesus. Suffering is the only criterion. Race and gender
are unimportant in God's eyes, even though, regrettably, they still seem
important to many of his followers.

I remember years ago being asked by The Leprosy Mission to visit the
Himalayan Kingdom of Bhutan. Its government had asked the Mission for
help with its leprosy problem. I travelled with two experienced senior
Indian Christian doctors. We faced the mountain roads together, by jeep
when we could, by foot and pony when the road disappeared. We found
many sufferers with neglected and serious leprosy, untreated because there
was no-one to treat them. Negotiating with the government, we were told
very firmly that they knew we were Christian, but while they would
welcome our medical care we would not be allowed to evangelise. In our
report to the Mission we recognised the restriction and recommended that
we accept it and begin work there anyway.

We were criticised by some well-meaning conservative Christians who
thought that we shouldn't enter the country if we were not free to
evangelise. My response was that it seemed to be a sad lack of compassion
to refuse people in great need the only opportunity of medical care they
would have, simply because of their government's restrictions on our
preaching. The Mission began work. Years later, leprosy is under control
in Bhutan, with very few new cases appearing, and with a growing band
of believers. A hand held out to heal is a clear witness in itself. Something
Jesus shows us.

But the centurion is aware of tensions as Jesus heads for his Gentile home.
"Lord," he says, "there's no need for you to go into my house. I don't
deserve it. You can heal him from here." In Jesus he recognises an

authority similar to his own, but greater. He can tell people to come and go, and he recognises the same power in Jesus. The elders had told Jesus that the centurion deserved Jesus' help, but the man himself realises that he could never deserve it. A refreshing humility from the soldier. Fortunately, deserving or undeserving doesn't come into the picture, either for him or us. None of us deserves the love God offers. None can earn it. Given the invitation and the need, Jesus will come to us anyway. Sometimes though, he has to break through our roof if the invitation is a little slow in coming.

Deserve your love?
Who can deserve it, Lord?
There's nothing I can say or do
to earn your love.
I've tried so hard to follow you by rule,
nose down on duty's grindstone,
and all that happened
was my nose got very sore.
And, I suspect,
gave cause for some amusement
at my expense.

But when the laughter's over –
well-meant and not unkind –
the great thing is
you love me anyway.
A blessing undeserved.
Oops! There I go again, that word – deserve.

You offer love without reserve.
No rules apply, and no small print,
the weasel words too small to read
that list conditions that would make it void.
Just love.
Here for the taking.
A treasure
written with my name upon it.
A love that welcomes
all who come in faith.
Lord, I sit back,
breathless, at the wonder of it all.

When Jesus heard this, he was astonished, and said to those
following him, "I tell you the truth, I have not found anyone in Israel
with such great faith. I say to you that many will come from the east
and the west, and will take their places at the feast with Abraham,
Isaac and Jacob in the kingdom of heaven."

Matthew 8:10-11

I can see the smile on Jesus' face as he hears the centurion's words. The
slow change of expression, the warmth in his eyes, the upturn at the
corners of his lips. I feel his heart leaping for joy as he recognises the
depth of faith in a Gentile outsider. This soldier, tough and unsentimental,
has recognised an authority in Jesus, so much greater than his own. And
from a different source. Jesus has faced doubt and criticism from his own
people; even anger. They were, supposedly, eagerly awaiting their coming
Messiah, yet unable or unwilling to recognise him in Jesus.

Jesus is amazed at the centurion's perception. His affirmation of Jesus
strengthens them both. He's made his leap of faith. Like the good soldier
he is, he steps out into the unknown, confident, not in his own strength,
but in the authority and character of the man standing in front of him.
He's committed, just as he would commit himself and his soldiers into
battle. Jesus delights in him, responds to him and without hesitation
opens the doors of the coming kingdom to him. Not because of what he'd
done in building the synagogue, not because he deserved it, but because of
his faith.

Jesus' next words are meant for the Jews, and he doesn't spare them. He
tells them that he's found more faith in this Gentile than in all Israel,
among God's chosen people. They were deeply shocked. Again, Jesus
questions their received teaching. Abraham, Isaac and Jacob were their
nation's honoured forefathers, key figures in the history and faith of the
Jewish people. The elders would understand their significance, whether
the Roman did or not. They believed that in the last days only they, as the
chosen people, would be accepted at the great feast in the community of
heaven. That barred all Gentiles. To suggest that the greatest faith Jesus
had encountered should have been seen in a Roman was shocking enough,
but that he and people of all races might be welcomed into the kingdom
stretched their understanding past its breaking point. Their welcome
would be on the same terms as anyone else's – on faith, not on birth,
privilege or rules. A sensational statement, met with gasps of incredulity.
But the love of God in Jesus breaks through the barriers we construct.
No-one is outside the compass of his love.

I'm attracted by the word *feast*. Jesus tells us that our welcome, our homecoming, won't be a formal affair, but a feast. A great and joyful celebration full of laughter. Feast comes from the Latin *festa* – joyous. A sort of *Marriage at Cana* feast, where the wine's always the best, and it never runs dry. And it will be full of surprising encounters with people we never expected to see, but all are welcome in this joyous community of heaven.

I don't know what the immediate future held for the centurion. His faith may have alienated him from his orthodox Jewish friends in the synagogue, but I see him making new bonds with the small group of believers who would meet in Peter's home. Sometimes I let my imagination run loose, and I see him cashing in his army career, if that was possible, and joining the disciples around Jesus. Perhaps getting them to walk a bit more smartly, to dress better, and his slave, fit and well, perhaps given his freedom. Or maybe Jesus told the centurion what he told other folk he'd helped, "Stay where you are, and tell the folk around you what God has done for you." (Luke 8:38-39) And the centurion, the good soldier, would hear and obey. Only God knows what really happened. But no-one who truly encounters Jesus is ever the same again.

We all need affirmation, Lord,
the encouragement that keeps us going
when we feel low.
And, dare I say it,
even you?
When ice-cold criticism
started to pile up in drifts around you,
you must have felt the need
for something warm.
A word from someone
telling you he understood.
A flash of eyes, quick meeting,
an eyebrow raised,
not to oppose
but as a sign he'd grasped the truth –
so beautiful a truth –
of what you'd said and done.
And when it came
from such an unexpected source,
I reckon that your heart just leapt with joy.
And, as you realised
the coming kingdom's boundaries
were wide enough to welcome him,
you laughed in sheer delight.
First at his faith,
then at the Father's love.
And I too share the joy,
amazed that I am welcome too,
not for my strength of faith or love,
but simply that I offer you
a resting place in me.

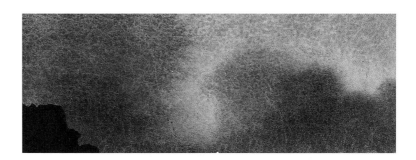

Passing Rain

Part Three
Calm after the Storm

Watercolour

Reading – Luke 8: 26-39

They sailed to the region of the Gerasenes, which is across the lake from Galilee. When Jesus stepped ashore, he was met by a demon-possessed man from the town. For a long time this man had not worn clothes or lived in a house, but had lived in the tombs. When he saw Jesus, he cried out and fell at his feet, shouting at the top of his voice, "What do you want with me, Jesus, Son of the Most High God? I beg you, don't torture me!" For Jesus had commanded the evil spirit to come out of the man. Many times it had seized him, and though he was chained hand and foot and kept under guard, he had broken his chains and had been driven by the demon into solitary places.

Jesus asked him, "What is your name?"
"Legion," he replied, because many demons had gone into him. And they begged him repeatedly not to order them to go into the Abyss.

A large herd of pigs was feeding there on the hillside. The demons begged Jesus to let them go into them, and he gave them permission. When the demons came out of the man, they went into the pigs, and the herd rushed down the steep bank into the lake and was drowned.

When those tending the pigs saw what had happened, they ran off and reported this in the town and countryside, and the people went out to see what had happened. When they came to Jesus, they found the man from whom the demons had gone out, sitting at Jesus feet, dressed and in his right mind; and they were afraid. Those who had seen it told the people how the demon-possessed man had been cured. Then all the people of the region of the Gerasenes asked Jesus to leave them, because they were overcome with fear. So he got into the boat and left.

The man from whom the demons had gone out begged to go with him, but Jesus sent him away, saying, "Return home and tell how much God has done for you." So the man went away and told all over the town how much Jesus had done for him.

Imagine...

They're wet, cold and tired. They lower the sail as the boat glides in under its own momentum. The keel grates on the shingle. Peter and Andrew, their robes tucked into their belts, jump out into knee-deep water and haul the boat a few inches further up the beach. They stand there while Jesus and the others disembark. It's unknown territory. They look around – a small beach hemmed in by limestone cliffs. A rocky path twists its way up to the cliff top. A few caves stand blank and dark, carved by sea and erosion. No-one in sight.

A quiet day is all they want; time to recover from the storm, and to reflect on all they'd seen and heard in and around Capernaum. Things hard to believe, even after seeing them with their own eyes. And did Jesus' power over human sickness extend to nature? Was it coincidence that the storm stopped at just the moment he told it to? Who was this man who'd called them? Who called them in such a way that they couldn't refuse, his words so compelling that they left everything to follow him. A quiet day, time to unwind, although they'd avoid the caves – evil spirits could live in them.

Then, suddenly, without warning, from the darkness of a cave a screaming, violent, naked presence rushes down towards them. Long matted hair and beard, skin grey with dirt, he shrieks and leaps, falls over and scrambles back to his feet, staring and breathless. His broken chains wind and unwind around his arms and feet as he runs, wrists and ankles red raw, scarred and bleeding. He's a fearful sight, his presence less than human, terrible and threatening. In that first moment Peter instinctively takes a step forward, and stands in front of Jesus to shield and defend him. John takes his place close by Jesus' side. The others each take a step back towards the boat. One picks up an oar for protection.

The man, possessed by forces he can't control, stands and screams incoherent curses. Jesus puts his hand firmly on Peter's shoulder, presses him aside. Jesus waits and suddenly the man sinks to his knees, sobbing, his words rushing out in a breathless plea for help. Then Jesus speaks. "What is your name?" Jesus recognises his humanity, tries to make contact. The struggle inside the man is fearful, the storm within frightening. The disciples look at each other, at the man, at Jesus. What will happen next?

*They sailed to the region of the Gerasenes,
which is across the lake from Galilee.*

Luke 8:26

Soon after his encounter with the Roman centurion, Jesus leaves
Capernaum and sails to Gentile territory. Matthew identifies it as the
region of the Gaderenes. Mark and Luke say Gerasenes. Maybe their
geography was a little patchy, but Matthew ought to have known. As an
ex-tax and customs collector in Capernaum, we could expect him to
know his geography a little better, even though his authority didn't
extend to that region. Apart from the puzzle over the exact location,
I find it difficult to work out the timing of this episode. Mark's Gospel
gives us a clue. He says that they set sail "That day when evening came."
(Mark 4: 35) Matthew and Luke give us no indication of time. There was
enough breeze to move the boat and keep it under control or they
wouldn't have sailed, and they'd reckon there was just enough light to get
them to their destination. But the easy journey was disrupted by a sudden
squall. Galilee is beautiful in the sunshine. I've sailed on it. But it's mood
can change rapidly. This storm was powerful enough to frighten even
experienced fishermen, and soon they were fighting for their lives in the
growing darkness.

But their later encounter with the demon-possessed man must have been a
daytime event. The report tells of a herd of pigs grazing – at night they
would have been safely penned in – and we're told that the herders saw all
that had happened. Then, as the story unfolds, they have time to alert the
pigs' owners in the town and bring them to see for themselves.

Yet I can't see Jesus and his crew taking all night to cross the lake; the
journey from Capernaum could only have been 12 or 15 miles. Could
they have been blown off course and delayed by the storm, or was the
wind and water so calm after Jesus had stilled them that they had to row?
Maybe they just rested and slept. Perhaps the timing was unimportant to
the gospel writers. They were intent on putting together two incidents
which spoke in dramatic form of Jesus' powers. Power to control external
events like the storm at sea, and also the internal, spiritual storms that
threaten to overwhelm the man with the demons.

Whatever the time of day, it must have been a shattering event for the
disciples, one totally outside their experience. Whether we accept the
diagnosis of demon possession, or try to identify it as a psychiatric
condition, the man is deeply disturbed and disturbing, and in need of

immediate help. The disciples were beginning to learn, as we all have to learn, that following Jesus isn't always a gentle stroll through the park. It can be a demanding, sometimes dangerous and frightening journey. The only assurance we have is his presence with us. We all have storms to weather in our journey, maybe not with the drama of these events, but disturbing to us. We need to be in touch with the power that can control them, the power we experience in Jesus. All we can do is stay close, as they did.

Looking back, Lord,
on their lives,
and trying to remember all the detail
as they told their stories later,
this can't have been the best day
that they'd had.
Not one they would recall with total satisfaction.
O yes, they had survived the storm at sea,
in which, so scared,
they'd nearly lost their lives.
And then the confrontation with the man
who scared them even more.

The outcome
scared them yet again.
When, looking at each other
as they questioned
what they were doing
following this man,
they asked themselves
why they'd left everything
to go with him.

I know the feeling, Lord.
In earlier, rosier days
the path seemed straight
and you were near
each time I called in faith.
But now, older and more tired,
and really not much wiser,
I sometimes ask the questions
the disciples asked.
You frighten me,
ask so much more than I can give,
or think I can.
I'm still committed,
I'll not give up,
abandon all I've lived by,
it's just I'd like a few less bumps
along the road.
My comfort is
in finding strength enough
to get me through the day.
And, come to think of it,
the strength must come from you.
So thank you, anyway.
I'll carry on, just for today.
Tomorrow's in your hands.

Lord of calm and storm,
I come to you for peace of mind.

On the Marsh, Norfolk

Watercolour

When Jesus stepped ashore, he was met by a demon-possessed man from the town. For a long time this man had not worn clothes or lived in a house, but had lived in the tombs.

Luke 8:27

They've sailed through the night and reached shore. It's morning. But it's foreign territory, Gentile country; there would have been no herds of pigs in Jewish Capernaum. It was part of the Decapolis, ten cities forming a loose alliance for trade and protection. We don't know why Jesus had brought them there. Was it deliberate choice or just the nearest landing place after the storm? But the beach leading up to the cliffs was deserted. The early morning sun was in their eyes, bright and warm, as they hauled the boat higher up the shingle, but the caves were dark, shadowy, unwelcoming. Folk used caves as tombs; they believed them to be places where ghosts and the spirits of the dead roamed. Frightening places, and the only people who sheltered there were outcasts, leprosy sufferers, the insane.

Now maybe the travellers can relax. All is calm and quiet. Yet the calm lasts only a minute – they don't even have time to unwrap the bread for breakfast. There's a terrifying scream and a shouting, raving, naked figure rushes at them from the caves. Jews were very uptight about nakedness – something they passed on to the Christian church. Instinctively, they freeze at his appearance. The man is alone – although Matthew says there were two men – take your pick. He's emaciated, grey with encrusted dirt, a great mane of hair and a matted beard, the scars and wounds from the chains and his own self-harm telling their story.

His community had done what it could to control him and to protect themselves. It's hard to lay blame on the blacksmith who'd fashioned the chains, or the authority that had ordered their use, or his family who could no longer cope with him, but there was a string of decisions all building up to his total rejection by folk who could have been more caring. Where were his guards? They might have helped him, or prevented at least some of his self-harm. A man deeply disturbed mentally and emotionally. Perhaps in his more lucid moments he had tried to end his life, to end the nightmare he was living. He was more threatened than threatening, more harmed than harming, and the community's attempts to control him only provoked him to increased violence, added fuel to the fire. We don't know whether he'd been banished deliberately to the tombs or whether he'd drifted there to avoid more suffering, but he was outcast, without hope.

Twenty-first Century doctors describe people deeply disturbed in mind and spirit in psychiatric terms. In Jesus' day, their suffering was attributed to demons, evil spirits. Their reality was never questioned. However we understand them, in Biblical times demons were a living and malevolent presence. They waited among tombs and lurked in the wilderness looking for new victims. Evil spirits are still feared in many societies today.

During my life in India, managing a large leprosy hospital, I remember one patient who believed he was under the control of an evil spirit. He became desperately afraid to sleep, was hysterical and uncontrollable. He threatened violence, then withdrew into a world of his own; but in his more lucid moments he pleaded for help and release. With appropriate medication, prayer and loving care, he lived through his ordeal and came out the other side. Whatever the psychiatrists might have said, or diagnosed, to him the evil spirit was real. The storm the disciples had experienced at sea had been frightening enough. Now the violence of the storm takes on a new dimension in human form.

Lord of calm and storm,
I come to you for peace of mind.
I don't ask that you still each storm I face,
I recognise that life's a mix of light and dark
to make me grow –
the same with plants –
although I wish you'd slow the rate
the grass grows on my lawn.

Life can be frightening,
the storms come out of nowhere,
but what I ask is just a little equanimity,
the ability to take life as it comes,
with some appreciation of the sunny days,
a mite less screaming when I face the dark.

You call it faith, I know,
the warm acceptance of your love,
the confidence that knows you're with me
in the dark as well as in the light.
The trust that reassures me
that everything will turn out right,
although it takes a little longer
than I could wish.
Shore up my faith, Lord,
strengthen my trust.
In asking that
it seems I'm asking you to do the work
and, in a way, I am.
I can't do anything alone.
It's only when you take up residence in me
that good things happen.
All I can do is say, "I'm grateful".

Jesus asked him, "What is your name?" " Legion," he replied,
because many demons had gone into him. And they begged him
repeatedly not to order them to go into the Abyss.

Luke 8: 30-31

Jesus is the one stable figure in the picture. He doesn't distance himself, or step back into the boat. He stands still. He makes no threatening or defensive movement to disturb the man who screams out again, or perhaps it was the spirits controlling him. Some commentators think that a slightly different order seems to clarify the event. They suggest that we should read v30 before v28. That would put Jesus' question, "What is your name?" right at the beginning, sparking off the whole confrontation. Reports can get confused. I imagine the disciples trying to piece together the whole incident afterwards. It had taken them by surprise, and their memories differed. "Do you remember the way he rushed at us? The yelling and screaming?" asked one. "Yes, then the Master asked his name..." said another, "No, that came later." And so on.

The man had little power against the spirits who tormented him, and it was they who gave him the physical strength to break his chains and frighten his guards away. Whichever way the confrontation continued, the demons scream out again. How did they recognise Jesus' authority and nature? A mystery we can't answer. "Don't torture us," they beg. It was a man at war with himself, the stress tearing him apart. I believe though that God never totally abandons anyone. We're told, "the Spirit helps us in our weakness. We do not know what we ought to pray for, but the Spirit himself intercedes for us with groans that words cannot express." (Romans 8:26) And I suggest it was this spirit of goodness still at work within the man, fighting hard against the demonic activity, that brought him to Jesus. Why else would he have come?

Then comes the response. "My name is Legion." Jesus, I believe, was asking the man for his own name, not the spirits'. They are trying to divert the conversation away from its centre, from their victim, while Jesus is trying to establish a relationship with the man himself. Getting him to say his name would be a first important step to halting his confusion and the disintegration of his personality. Names are important. They show our individuality, and God loves us as individuals. Saint Augustine wrote, 'God loves each of us as if we were the only person on earth, yet God loves all as God loves each.'

The Long and Winding Road

Your life, your love, entice me,
draw me from the little world
I recognise as mine
and set me on the path
you'd have me take.

Watercolour

The name the demons give intrigues me. Legion. A legion was a regiment of Roman soldiers, the hated occupiers of the land. As Roman legions had taken control of Israel, so the spirits had taken control of this man's personality. Both Romans and demons were feared and hated by the people, and some must have enjoyed the thought of a Roman legion entering a herd of unclean pigs and drowning in the lake. I wonder, too, if the name 'Legion' suggests a possible reason for the man's deep disturbance? Although this area of the Gerasenes was not controlled directly by Rome, it had been overrun by its legions. Had the man had some dreadful experience with them, or been a victim of their violence in a way that opened him up, made him vulnerable, to whatever had seized him?

"Don't torture us," they pleaded. But they had tortured their host – why should they expect mercy for themselves? So often, when challenged, the bully is a *frightened* rather than a *frightening* figure. They too are fearful – of the Abyss, a place of desolation where they would be cut off from God and all goodness. They prefer the pigs, but that won't save them in the end.

Just a country lane, Lord,
full of sheep.
I was impatient –
not unusual, I must admit –
and all those woolly animals
just milling aimlessly around,
annoyed me,
while I was waiting to get on.
A shepherd and two dogs
were in control.
I would admire their training
in other circumstances,
but they were in my way.

And then, sheep all around my car,
I thought of you, Lord –
shepherd, sheep –
I'm sure you get the picture,
and I wondered
if that shepherd's sheep had names.
I doubt it,
there could be so little time or space in memory.
Too many sheep, too many names,
for one man to remember.
But then I thanked you, Lord,
and do so now.
Your memory holds the world,
our names, in love.
My name included, valued,
in your book of life.
When problems come
and darkness threatens,
my balance not the best,
your hand is near to steady me
and help me take another step.
I thank you, yet again.

When they came to Jesus, they found the man from whom the
demons had gone out, sitting at Jesus feet, dressed and in his right
mind; and they were afraid. Those who had seen it told the people
how the demon-possessed man had been cured. Then all the people
of the region of the Gerasenes asked Jesus to leave them, because
they were overcome with fear. So he got into the boat and left.

Luke 8:35-37

"Then all the people ... asked Jesus to leave..." The saddest phrase in the
story. They were scared by the awesome power they'd seen in Jesus and
their reaction was to distance themselves from it. I have some sympathy
with the pig owners. They'd done nothing wrong to deserve the loss of
both their capital and income; and if Jesus used the pigs deliberately to
allow the spirits to enter them, it puzzles me because it hardly shows the
care and compassion which were at the root of his nature. Commentators
sometimes suggest that there was some other event that frightened the
pigs into a stampede – do pigs stampede? – and that Jesus, seeing it in
the distance, used it, and clothed his healing in the language and beliefs
of his time. "Look," he says, shaking the now nearly inert man by the
shoulder and pointing, "there are your demons, they've gone, just as the
pigs have gone. You're free." A graphic picture that could help the man
back to reality.

The herders panic too. They're responsible for the pigs, which would no
doubt be counted in and out each day. They rush back through the
villages nearby to the town, shouting news of the catastrophe. "It wasn't
our fault." I'm sure that more than one startled pig owner must have
thought the story was a very imaginative excuse to avoid blame for losing
their charges. And the people, the pig owners and the curious, stream
down to the shore line. Some pause at the cliff top and look down, others
scramble down the path and gape.

Jesus is quietly reassuring the man, to whom a rapidly gathering crowd is still menacing. The man himself is quiet, clothed, but a little apprehensive. I wonder who led the man down to the water's edge and began to scrub him clean? Which disciple rummaged through his bundle of clothes and offered a robe? And who found that little phial of oil and began to dress the man's wounds? By this time, I think he would have been in tears, letting out some of the years of suffering and fear, and moved by this unexpected care. And in his right mind – something God wills for each one of us: to be in our right minds. Someone said that 'our sinful self is not our true self.' Jesus straightens out our values, challenges us to become the fully integrated human beings God created us to be.

I wonder, in passing, if this experience later inspired Jesus to tell his story of the lost son and the forgiving father. After the prodigal had lost everything and was reduced to herding pigs – pigs again – we're told 'he came to his senses.' (Luke 15:17) We're never complete, never fulfilled, until we find a way to the wholeness Jesus offers. And he offered it without conditions to this deeply disturbed man. There was no talk of faith – the man wasn't sufficiently in control of his own life to make that leap, but now he can. His contact with Jesus sets him free. Free to regain his dignity and make choices.

That doesn't seem to be the way the townsfolk saw it. "It's all very well looking after him, the man who's made life miserable for us, but what about our pigs? He may be all right but we've lost money." And they ask Jesus to leave. His power, used only in love, frightens them. They can see no further than their balance sheets. A message for today. They've seen the change for good in the life of the man possessed, but they're afraid of the change Jesus might bring to their own lives. What an opportunity missed. Jesus doesn't argue. Sadly, and almost as an anticlimax, he follows the others into the boat. Again, Peter and Andrew push it into deeper water and they leave.

In his right mind, Lord,
all passion spent.
I wonder, did he recollect
the fearful nightmare he'd been through?
His life, the battlefield
on which a struggle had been fought
by ill and good,
hatred and love.
And as he sat
still and quiet on the beach,
did he remember and give thanks?
Now he was free,
his mind restored.

Free from the chains of pain and fear
that held him captive,
stronger than the chains he'd broken
not so long ago.
Free now to take a grip on life,
on all you offered,
and begin again.

And now, like him,
I would begin again.
I look to you for healing
and renewal of my mind.
Not for the first time, Lord.
My promises pass their sell-by-date
more rapidly than I would wish,
but now
I'm ready to move on.

The man from whom the demons had gone out begged to go with him, but Jesus sent him away, saying, "Return home and tell how much God has done for you." So the man went away and told all over the town how much Jesus had done for him.

Luke 8:38-39

The man, now restored and in his right mind, "stands at the grave's entrance and rubs death from his eyes".* Then, standing on the beach, he pleads to go with Jesus. To go with the one who'd never feared or rejected him. The one who'd given him a new start, new life. "Look," he gestures, "there's room in the boat for another one. Let me come. I'm scared. I don't want to stay here." Jesus refuses, tells him to stay where he is. "Go home," he says. Mark's Gospel adds, " to your family" (Mark 5:19), although they'd been notably absent so far. I'm sure that whatever Jesus' exact words were, they were said firmly, but gently.

The man turns and faces the remnant of the crowd who don't yet know how to deal with him. Some just stare or make comments, others move away. One questions him. "Well then, what happened? What did he do to you? What are you going to do now?" Another, braver than the rest, reaches out and touches him.

What to do next? I'm not sure how the man faced this question. Maybe in the few moments quiet he'd had with Jesus after his healing, and before the crowd appeared, Jesus had encouraged him, strengthened his damaged confidence. We're not told how any of the folk Jesus restored to health faced their immediate future. His presence and power brought healing, but also the need to face changed circumstances, to make a new start, to take hold of life and its responsibilities. For this man it's a resurrection. An ancient Christian teacher said that the work of resurrection goes on in us all the time as we live and grow and develop.**

The man walks through the crowd and begins the climb up the path to the cliff top and beyond, not yet sure how he'll take up his life again. Following Jesus isn't always easy.

* R.S. Thomas
** Theophilus of Antioch, 2nd Century AD.

We're not usually given detailed instructions about our corner of life, just guiding principles on which to base our own decisions. That's as true for him as it is for us. He's told to go home, and given a job to do. He's sent back to his family and community to tell what God had done for him. This is often the most difficult task we have – to witness to our own community – but that's what most of us are called to do. To stay where we are and tell others what God has done, and is doing, in our lives, and to point others in the direction of Jesus. The people had rejected Jesus, told him to go, but he doesn't abandon them. The man stays there as Jesus' ambassador, his representative, who will talk about his meeting with Jesus for the rest of his life. Note that Jesus tells him to talk about what *God* has done for him, but he goes out and tells what *Jesus* has done. Now in his right mind, he recognises the one element of truth in the demons' words: that God and Jesus are inseparable. And he is left to face the pressures of his world in the strength of Jesus. For him, and for us, 'Nothing in life is certain, but everything is safe.'*

And the disciples? They're even more amazed, disturbed, bewildered. They're beginning to see Jesus not simply as an inspired and charismatic teacher – as many would accept him today – but as a man whose absolute closeness to God, whom he called Father, gave him an authority and power never seen before or since. They see Jesus now breaking through the partition between the physical and spiritual worlds, and extending the boundaries of his compassion beyond anything they might have thought possible. God's love is no longer the possession of one nation, and all are welcome – a Roman centurion, and pagan Gadarenes.

Charles Williams

Lord, it seems to me
that resurrection comes
in many ways.

It lurks around the corners of my life,
waits quietly,
sets roots,
shoots leaves,
then blossoms into beauty
which makes me gasp.

Sometimes I'm slow to take it up.
I'd rather live in yesterday,
the known,
its challenge stale,
than face the excitement still to come.

But you persist
I'm glad to say.
Your life, your love, entice me,
draw me from the little world
I recognise as mine
and set me on the path
you'd have me take.

I take it nervously at times
in face of the unknown,
but trusting I'll meet you again
along the way.
I know I will
but if I seem a little shaky, Lord,
I'm sure my confidence will grow.

Spring Lilies

Part Four

Breaking Through into Life

Watercolour

Reading – Luke 8:40-56

Now when Jesus returned, a crowd welcomed him, for they were all expecting him. Then a man named Jairus, a ruler of the synagogue, came and fell at Jesus' feet, pleading with him to come to his house because his only daughter, a girl of about twelve, was dying.

As Jesus was on his way, the crowds almost crushed him. And a woman was there who had been subject to bleeding for twelve years, but no-one could heal her. She came up behind him and touched the edge of his cloak, and immediately her bleeding stopped.
"Who touched me?" Jesus asked.
When they all denied it, Peter said, "Master, the people are crowding and pressing against you."
But Jesus said, "Someone touched me; I know that power has gone out from me."

Then the woman, seeing that she could not go unnoticed, came trembling and fell at his feet. In the presence of all the people, she told why she had touched him and how she had been instantly healed. Then he said to her, "Daughter, your faith has healed you. Go in peace."

While Jesus was still speaking, someone came from the house of Jairus, the synagogue ruler. "Your daughter is dead," he said. "Don't bother the teacher any more."
Hearing this, Jesus said to Jairus, " Don't be afraid; just believe, and she will be healed."

When he arrived at the house of Jairus, he did not let anyone go in with him except Peter, John and James, and the child's father and mother. Meanwhile, all the people were wailing and mourning for her. "Stop wailing," Jesus said, "She is not dead but asleep."

They laughed at him, knowing that she was dead. But he took her by the hand and said, "My child, get up!" Her spirit returned and at once she stood up. Then Jesus told them to give her something to eat. Her parents were astonished, but he ordered them not to tell anyone what had happened.

Imagine...

Crowds again, always crowds. The disciples have mixed feelings about crowds. This one is welcoming and eager, folk pushing to see and hear Jesus, and to ask for his help. People bringing their problems, their hopes, with one thing in common: that they needed a grace and power beyond their own to reach out and touch their lives. It wasn't like the crowd they'd just experienced on the other side of the lake: an angry mob, frightened and upset, who'd told Jesus starkly that he wasn't wanted there.

The disciples were beginning to realise Jesus' unique qualities, and to wonder at the wisdom and power that drew many people to him, but the throng is demanding, tiring. They're having to fight their way through from the beach to the road. They're proud to be with him but sometimes the sheer physical effort of pushing through and protecting him is exhausting. After all, they're only human.

It's hot and dry in the narrow streets of Capernaum, and the dust kicked up by the constant movement of many people hits the back of their throats, gets in their hair, mingles with the pervading smell of hot, struggling bodies. Noise too. Shouting. It might almost be a riot. What will the soldiers think - the Romans, here to keep the peace? The noise persists as they slowly move on. It's mostly an unintelligible jumble of shouts as many voices call out at the same time, each one desperate to be heard. It's confusion. Then, people fall back a little as one man fights his way to Jesus. It's Jairus, a leader in the local synagogue. He's respectable and respected, and those nearest in the crowd try to give him a little space. He looks anxious and uncomfortable. Usually, he'd never dream of pushing into a gathering like this. But this isn't usual. His daughter's sick, dying, his only daughter, the light of his life. He's tried everything, but the doctors have given up. He's weighed down by anxiety and grief, but that same grief drives him to do the unthinkable: to ask Jesus for help.

The noise lessens a little, as those near the action see them meeting. Then shocked surprise. Jairus falls to his knees. It could have been accidental, a foot catching his ankle but no, Jairus is on his knees in front of Jesus, hands out in supplication. He forgets the people watching, thinks nothing of his own lack of dignity. This is no time to be embarrassed. "Please," he sobs. "Please help me. There's no-one else I can ask." He's desolate. The people wait. A few more words, then Jesus helps him to his feet. Jairus leads the way home, just ahead of Jesus, looking back all the time, willing him to hurry.

They've only gone a few metres when there's another stir in the crowd. Jesus stops and speaks to his disciples. He looks concerned. Jairus beckons him on, urgently pointing ahead, but Jesus' attention is now elsewhere. As he turns he starts to speak to a woman. A woman? In this crowd of men? Unusual to say the least. Shocking. She looks unsure of herself, her body language betrays her. She's nervous, deferential, her shoulders hunched, head bowed. Only Jesus can hear her muttered words but suddenly her face lights up. She straightens up, her shoulders high, a smile of pure joy on her face. Then, still smiling her thanks, she slips away, swallowed by the throng.

Jairus waits, his expression changing from hope to impatience and despair. He wonders if he dare take Jesus by the arm, or pull at his cloak to get him moving again. But no, he can't do that, even though the woman had. "Please," he murmurs, "it's not far. Please."

Now when Jesus returned, a crowd welcomed him, for they were all expecting him. Then a man named Jairus, a ruler of the synagogue, came and fell at Jesus' feet, pleading with him to come to his house because his only daughter, a girl of about twelve, was dying.

Luke 8:40-42

The crowd's welcome lifted their spirits after the Gadara people's anger and rejection. The disciples are happy to be back in familiar surroundings after their adventures over on the other side of the lake. They have much to tell – although they'll have to be careful how they mention the pigs. But first they feel they can relax. This is their own beach, their home town, for some of them anyway. What now? The crowd's excited and growing every minute. Friendly but demanding. People asking, begging, for Jesus' attention.

There's a stir as Jairus struggles through the people. He's a worthy man, one with influence in the small town of Capernaum. He's a ruler of the synagogue, his duties to arrange the Sabbath services and invite the speakers. Had he chaired the earlier meeting when Jesus was invited to speak? Was he there when Jesus cast out the evil spirit? (Luke 4:31-37) Here he is now, pushing his way through to Jesus. Actually pushing, not waiting for others to move out of his way. I imagine the pressures on Jairus, a pillar of the establishment. He might well have been reluctant to ask Jesus, this controversial and unorthodox teacher, for any kind of help. Jesus wasn't quite an outsider yet, but his presence was becoming hard to handle. Yet his healing powers couldn't be ignored. I imagine that Jairus had met the centurion who'd built the synagogue, and that he'd heard of Jesus restoring his servant's health.

I'm sure Jairus' wife's tears, and his own deep love for his daughter, pushed him on. "His only daughter," says Luke. "His little daughter," says Mark 5:23. Did Jairus have any sons? It doesn't say his only child, simply his only daughter. She wasn't 'little' – she was rapidly approaching adult life and almost ready for marriage in the culture in which she lived, but she's still the light of her father's life. And she's dying.

I watched a real-life film on television about children with cystic fibrosis. One was a lovely 15-year-old girl, beautiful and articulate. She was waiting for a heart and lung transplant, and she understood clearly what would happen to her if it didn't come in time. It didn't. She died 11 days after the interview. The sadness and grief is just the same for any parent in this situation, no matter what century they live in. In Jesus' day, many people died young, life expectancy was low, but this daughter was special to her father Jairus, and her mother, and they can't let her go. Grief makes him desperate and he falls at Jesus' feet. Jesus asks no questions. The grief he sees is enough.

So easy, Lord, to crowd you out.
So much to do,
so little time to do it all.
I struggle through the crowd
of my own busyness
to get to you,
each little thing an obstacle delaying me.
And everything I need to do
coils round my feet
and trips me up.
Keeps us apart.

All that I need to do, Lord?
You question it –
why do I need to do so much?
Well then,
there's family and church
and all those other jobs
that fill my diary and...
You question me again.
But all I do, I do for you,
or try to anyway,
and if the quality's not very good
you could at least acknowledge
all the effort I put in.
But when I take a breath
and stop to think,
the very work I do for you
holds us apart.

And if I really love you,
as I say I do,
I'd push away the things
my ego thinks important
to spend more time
not working for,
but being with,
the one I say I love.
I think we'd both enjoy it more.

> She came up behind him and touched the edge of his cloak,
> and immediately her bleeding stopped.
> "Who touched me?" Jesus asked.
>
> Luke 8:44-45

Another interruption for Jesus to deal with. She shouldn't have been in this crowd at all, her presence polluted it. Her illness made her ceremonially unclean in a male-dominated society. Barred from the synagogue – Jairus' synagogue – she was cut off from all communal activities. An outcast. As much an outcast in her way as the man in Gadara. Yet she gathers up all her remaining strength and determination. She pushes in, desperate, heart pounding. She's heard of Jesus' healing power – there can't have been many in Capernaum who hadn't – and this is her only chance. A once-in-a-lifetime opportunity for healing. She has to take it, breaking through convention, risking everything to get to Jesus.

Her condition was chronic. She'd been sick for 12 years, the whole time Jairus' 12-year-old daughter had lived. She'd tried every remedy there was. Doctor Luke says simply, "No-one could heal her." Doctors are careful not to criticise each other. Mark's version is less restrained. He reports, "She had suffered a great deal under the care of many doctors and had spent all she had, yet instead of getting better she grew worse." (Mark 5:26) She'd gone from doctor to doctor, from hope to dashed hope. She'd spent everything, only to be disillusioned, her condition no better, even worse. She'd suffered unbearably. Seen her relationships shatter. But somehow, through what she's heard, she's convinced that this teacher can help. Desperation and faith come together.

She struggles through the throng. She can't approach him face to face, she's too ashamed, and so she comes to Jesus from behind. "Just to touch the edge of his cloak," she thinks. That's all she needs. Jesus stands still. It's ironic that the needs of this woman, excluded from Jairus' synagogue, now come before Jairus' needs.

Immediately – that word again, I love it – she's healed. We'll never understand how, we simply accept. Nor can we comprehend how Jesus knew someone had touched him, but he did. He stops, looks round, searches faces, and asks his question. The disciples are incredulous. "Come on," they say, "you're in a crowd, you're being touched all the time. We can't hold people back." True, but not all were touching him with the woman's faith. Jesus persists. "Someone touched me; I know that power has gone out from me." There's a vulnerability about Jesus.

There's a cost to him, to his energy, in his healings, and here we glimpse a little of what it meant.

My wife's been very ill. During her recovery, we eventually found a wonderful physiotherapist. She was concerned with Barbara not simply as a collection of muscles and nerves, but with the reaction of her whole mind and body to her illness. She treated Barbara as a complete person. The physio once said to me that "when she had finished a session treating a particularly needy patient she felt drained, as though all her energy had gone into the one she was treating." Jesus knew this feeling, I'm sure. The woman is now in the centre of the throng, conspicuous in a crowd of men. She realises that she'll be noticed. She's frightened, trembling. She has to confess. How will Jesus react? What will the crowd do? She falls at his feet – had she seen Jairus do that a few moments earlier? – and in a sudden rush of words she tells her story.

What a contrast they make – Jairus and the unnamed woman. He a well-respected member of the community, she outcast by her illness. He, we assume, comfortably off, she penniless, having spent all her money searching for a cure. He upright, sure of his place in both synagogue and community, she rejected by both. He 'righteous', she, without knowing why, feeling the guilt of some unknown sin for which she bears the shame. But in their mutual suffering they each place their trust in Jesus.

As always, Jesus reacts with love. He takes no account of her 'uncleanness', even though the law states that it would have been transferred to him by her touch, however slight. He breaks through centuries of deeply held male prejudice to accept her, and to draw her into his growing community of those who believe. He accepts her. "Daughter," he says, an affectionate and affirming word – just as he'd used "Son," to the paralysed man – "your faith has healed you." Then Jesus speaks words of assurance, "Go in peace and be freed from your suffering." (Mark 5:34) With the touch, so light, she emerges from the darkness and depression in which she's lived so long into the light of new life. The crowd make way for her as she begins this new life. Not 'takes up her old life' – that had long gone. Contact with Jesus, even for a moment, can change life totally. For the first time in 12 years she is at peace, a smile lighting up her face. How long had it been since she'd smiled?

Lord, I struggle to get close,
to see, and touch your robe.
I stand on tiptoe,
hoping for a glimpse
above the shoulders of my fears,
but crowding questions block my vision.
They hold me back,
however much I fight to clear a path,
my elbows sharpened by my desperation.
I envy those –
I know I'm not supposed to –
who seem to walk with you at every step.
Who slide into their faith with ease,
a perfect fit,
and wear their trust like medals
gleaming in the sunlight,
with just a tiny hint of pride.

Maybe their struggle, Lord,
is just as hard as mine,
it's just that I don't see it,
so forgive me if I oversimplify.
But then I hear
your voice again,
although it sounds like mine,
saying I overcomplicate the situation.
I'm just a bit confused.

And then I see you smile at last.
I hear you say
"It's really not as hard
as you would make it.
I'm always here for you.
Don't wait for questions to be answered,
just reach and touch."
And then my healing can begin.
My questions put aside
and I may go,
like her,
in peace.
I thank you, Lord.

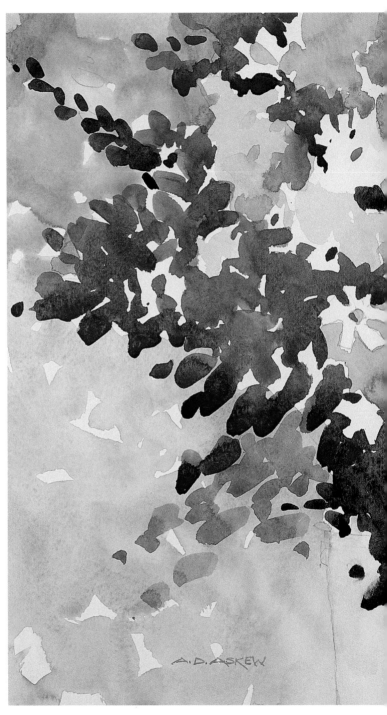

Riches of Summer

I'm bound to you
in freedom,
love's paradox.
The tighter that you hold,
the more the space
you offer me
to do it in my way.

Watercolour

> While Jesus was still speaking, someone came from the
> house of Jairus, the synagogue ruler. "Your daughter is dead,"
> he said. "Don't bother the teacher any more."
>
> Luke 8:49

"Go in peace," Jesus said to the woman. Jairus isn't at peace. He's agitated, moving from one foot to the other. It's all he can do not to take Jesus by the arm and pull him along. His daughter, his much loved only daughter, is dying. Dying. He screams inwardly at the delay. Every moment counts. He's hardly noticed the woman's healing; all he can do is wait impatiently, his desperation clear to see. His sole purpose is to get Jesus home as fast as he can. His shoulders sag, hope draining away through his feet. He's put so much faith in Jesus, but now what? Waiting, even the few minutes' pause here, is difficult. And for a woman?

She goes away, renewed in body and spirit. She's swallowed by the crowd, just ahead of the news of her healing, as it was passed from one man to the next. That was the good news, now comes the bad. Just as Jairus gets Jesus moving again, someone from his house finds him. The look on the messenger's face tells its story. "Your daughter is dead," he says. Stark, final words. "Don't bother the teacher any more." The messenger uses the word 'teacher', not 'healer'. A sad and dismissive phrase. There's no point anymore. He can't help. No-one can help. Jairus is near to collapse, his face distraught. Tears flow again. He looks at Jesus almost accusingly, and thinks, "If only you hadn't stopped."

Jesus offers hope even now. He sees Jairus' anguish. "Don't be afraid," he says, "hold on to your faith in me." He doesn't promise an easy ride in the daylight, but he promises to travel with us when times get dark. Hang on even in your desperation, it's brought you this far. It's not only his daughter who needs Jesus' touch, it's Jairus himself. Sue Monk Kidd writes about 'the desert between our wounds and our healing, our questions and our answers, our departures and our arrivals.'* Jesus can pour his love into Jairus' emptiness, into our emptiness. There have been many times when Jesus has had to say that to me. I've hung onto my faith by my fingertips, shouting questions but getting no direct answers. But somehow, in that moment of despair, Jesus is present in the crisis. All crises. Don't be afraid, even when our personal miseries drown the words.

* When the Heart Waits, *by Sue Monk Kidd. Harper Collins 1992*

We were singing a modern hymn in church. I have a mixed attitude to contemporary worship songs. Some are a great help and inspiration. Others, with poor grammar, badly mixed imagery and repetitive, uninspired melodies, turn me off. We were singing one with the words "And in the storm, your love is the anchor."* That phrase invaded my mind during worship, and for the next ten days it kept popping up totally out of my control. When I got up in the morning, or if I woke in the night, whenever, the words were there. My mind sang them repeatedly. I tried singing other songs, or changing the thought altogether. Nothing worked, it was a constant irritation. Then one day I thought, "Those words are meant for me. I need to accept them, not stick them in the garbage bin. Just hold on in the storm, love is the anchor you need."

Sometimes, I'm a slow learner. Life can be tough – it was for me at that time – and it may seem as though the Lord is too busy dealing with someone else's problems, rather than mine, but he's nearer than we think. "God is nearer to me than I am to myself," said Meister Eckhart.**

* Faithful One, So Unchanging, *by Brian Doerksen, Vineyard Music*
** Mysticism, *Chapter 5*

Love is the anchor, Lord.
The one sure thing
that holds me safe.

I'm bound to you in freedom,
love's paradox.
The tighter that you hold,
the more the space
you offer me
to do it in my way.

But always we adventure,
you and I,
sail on the ocean,
explore new lands, new roads,
new truth.
And when I'm scared
and feel I've gone too far,
my navigation faulty,
I look around
and you are there beside me.

Telling me
that when the storm clouds gather
and wind whips up,
to blow me in directions
I would not choose to go,
I have no cause to fear.

You are beside me,
yes, but strange,
ahead of me as well.
Love's landmark,
beacon blazing,
beckoning me on,
and promising safe anchorage.

Autumn Gold

I find some comfort
in familiar words,
like 'son' and 'daughter',
and 'my child'.
The words you use
to bring us lovingly
into your kingdom,
part of the family.

Watercolour

When he arrived at the house of Jairus, he did not let anyone go in
with him except Peter, John and James, and the child's father and
mother. Meanwhile all the people were wailing and mourning for
her. "Stop wailing," Jesus said." She is not dead but asleep." They
laughed at him, knowing that she was dead. But he took her by the
hand and said, "My child get up!"

Luke 8:51-54

Jairus goes through a catalogue of emotion. Anxiety, despair, impatience,
glimmers of hope, soon dashed. "What's the point?" Jairus asks himself,
"she's dead." He can hardly walk, he's near to collapse. But still Jesus
goes with him. They approach Jairus' house. There's uproar. Uninhibited
grief. Mourning for the tragedy of a 12-year-old's death. Jairus' going to
Jesus had been a last ditch effort, the final attempt to save her life. Yet
they were too late. Already the professional mourners were there, music
and all. (Matthew 8:23) Here's another storm. Jesus had stilled the storm
at sea, the storm in the mind of the sick man in Gadara, now he's faced
with commotion around and within Jairus' house. People approach Jairus
with sympathy, murmuring the platitudes. "It's all for a purpose, it's all
God's will." They don't help. Better to hold him and say nothing.

"She's asleep," says Jesus, reassuring them: except that he doesn't,
because they don't believe what he's saying. Their mourning turns to
derisive laughter. They'd seen the girl, Jesus hadn't. They knew the
difference between death and sleep. Death was commonplace and they
weren't prepared to accept his word.

Jesus needs quiet. He enters the house, pushes out the noisy ones. He
takes only three disciples in with him – maybe the others stood outside the
door and kept it shut? – and the girl's weeping mother and father. Jairus
stands with his wife, trembling. He's trying so hard to grasp the straw of
hope Jesus' words offer. Jesus takes the girl's hand, still warm. I think he
kneels to whisper gently into her ear. No loud, peremptory command; just
the gentle encouragement we give at the end of a long journey to a tired
child who's fallen asleep in the back seat of the car. A "Come on, love,
we're home," sort of voice. Perhaps her spirit had been on a long journey.
"Son" he'd said to the paralysed man. (Mark 5:41) "Daughter," to the
woman he'd healed a few minutes before. Now it's, "My child, get up."
Another loving, familiar word. We are each part of the family of God, his
community. Some have never strayed from it, others, like the prodigal,
have been far from home, but for all who look to Jesus, there's a loving
welcome on their return to the family.

The girl wakes. The first thing she sees? The face of a loving stranger, Jesus. Then her mother and father, who stand rooted for a second, then rush to embrace her. They must have pushed Jesus aside in the small room, but I don't think he'd mind. They're laughing and crying and murmuring to each other, while he stands in a corner and says a quiet prayer of thanksgiving. The girl doesn't understand this sudden outburst of joy, but she enjoys, or endures, the repeated hugs and kisses. The family is whole again.

Lord, it's easy to scoff.
Folk stand along the sidelines
watching.
Uncommitted.
To laugh at what or whom
they do not understand,
and say it's all a load of rubbish.
Throw stones of scorn –
that often bruise the thin skin of my faith.
And though I try to say
I bear it all for you
I sometimes wish
the stones would ricochet,
just now and then,
and hit them back.
I couldn't be accused of throwing them,
but I'd enjoy it just the same.

But when they've really hurt
and I sit back, wounds licked,
I find some comfort
in familiar words,
like 'son' and 'daughter',
and 'my child'.
The words you use
to bring us lovingly
into your kingdom,
part of the family.
An offer of new life.

I'll take it, Lord,
and if you're happy
I'll come in as your child,
alive as I have never been before,
eager to sing and play.
And there I'll find a peg,
my name already written on it,
on which I'll hang my love for you.

Her spirit returned, and at once she stood up. Then Jesus told them to give her something to eat. Her parents were astonished, but he ordered them not to tell anyone what had happened.

Luke 8:55-56

Jairus and his wife are reeling with the shock. All they can hold onto is their daughter. Too much is happening too quickly. In a moment they bounce from grief through incredulity to joy. They're out of their depth. They need an anchor, something to bring them down from the miracle to everyday life. Jesus offers it. "Give her something to eat," he says. But of course. That would bring them down to earth: mother anyway. Preparing food, feeding the family, was her everyday responsibility. It also reinforced the reality of what had happened – the dead don't eat. Bread is quickly broken, with perhaps a cup of watered wine. Bread and wine eaten in his presence. I wonder, did they offer some to Jesus?

"She's dead," the family messenger had said. "Don't trouble the teacher." The crowd of mourners who'd laughed at Jesus agreed. Today people say, "God is dead, we don't need him anymore." They laugh, and ridicule belief. But Jesus' presence and power is still a living reality. A reality which brings new life.

I reckon, though, that there were some things even Jesus couldn't control. He told Jairus and his wife to tell no-one what had happened, and I suggest that part of their astonishment was in wondering how they could keep it within the family. Or why? There was no way it could remain secret. Family and mourners had seen the dead girl. Soon, as she walked from the room and began to take up her life again, they'd see her alive. It would be impossible to keep it quiet. Jesus said the same to the leprosy sufferer he'd healed: "See that you don't tell this to anyone." (Mark 1:44) That didn't work either, and soon crowds were besieging him.

I try to picture the days ahead. To the girl it must have seemed to have happened to someone else. A dream. A story told around a fire in the courtyard on a dark evening. She only knew what she'd been told, and I hope that as her experience receded into the past, she'd be able to leave it at the back of her memory and lead a normal, happy life. But for Jairus she'd remain the one who'd been lost and found again.

I wonder too if their common experiences brought Jairus, the synagogue ruler, and the centurion who'd had a hand in building it, closer together. Both had come to Jesus with a mixture of anxiety and faith. Both had asked for the healing of someone else and had experienced Jesus' power. One of the loveliest things about contact with Jesus is the way he brings together people of different cultures and lifestyles. The established church isn't always as good at that as it should be. At times it seems quicker to exclude than to welcome folk with a different lifestyle, but the spirit of Christ is one that breaks through the barriers we humans set up in our weakness. St. Paul proclaims, "There is neither Jew nor Greek, slave nor free, male nor female, for you are all one in Christ Jesus." (Galatians 3:28)

Lord, I wonder
what her appetite was like.
How hungry was she
after an adventure
no-one here on earth
can ever know or visualise?
Breaking through the membrane
between life and death
and back again.

And did the food taste different
from anything she'd ever had before,
prepared by mother's hand,
still trembling
from the drama of the situation?
Food ordinary and everyday,
made special by the blessing
of your presence.

And good old Jairus –
was he, exhausted now,
still sitting on the bed his child had left,
his tears and laughter,
one so like the other?

And you, Lord?
Smiling that secret smile
that mirrored heaven's joy
at life renewed,
and willing them to find you
in the ordinary things of life.

Miracles are great
but happen not so often
that they might lose their impact -
that's why we call them miracles, I suppose -
but finding and identifying you
in all the bread-and-butter things,
the bread and wine of everyday activity.
Your living, loving presence
in the day's routine,
sparking to joy each thing I do.

Morning Flight

Part Five

Walking Away?

Watercolour

Reading – Luke 18:15-30

People were also bringing babies to Jesus to have him touch them. When the disciples saw this, they rebuked them. But Jesus called the children to him and said, "Let the little children come to me, and do not hinder them, for the kingdom of God belongs to such as these. I tell you the truth, anyone who will not receive the kingdom of God like a little child will never enter it."

A certain ruler asked him, "Good teacher, what must I do to inherit eternal life?" "Why do you call me good?" Jesus answered. "No-one is good – except God alone. You know the commandments: Do not commit adultery, do not murder, do not steal, do not give false testimony, honour your father and your mother."

"All these I have kept since I was a boy," he said. When Jesus heard this, he said to him, "You still lack one thing. Sell everything you have and give to the poor, and you will have treasure in heaven. Then come, follow me."

When he heard this, he became very sad, because he was a man of great wealth. Jesus looked at him and said, "How hard it is for the rich to enter the kingdom of God! Indeed, it is easier for a camel to go through the eye of a needle than for a rich man to enter the kingdom of God." Those who heard this asked, "Who then can be saved?" Jesus replied, "What is impossible with men is possible with God."

Peter said to him, "We have left all we had to follow you!" "I tell you the truth," Jesus said to them, "no-one who has left home or wife or brothers or parents or children for the sake of the kingdom of God will fail to receive many times as much in this age and, in the age to come, eternal life."

Reading – Mark 10:21

Jesus looked at him and loved him.

Imagine...

It must have been difficult to choose a birthday present for the rich young ruler. He has everything. There he stands, well dressed, his white robe the purest, softest, best woven wool that traders could sell. His hair and beard well groomed. His finger nails clean – unlike those of Jesus and his disciples. He's never planed wood, or heaved heavy fishing nets, or gutted fish. His skin is oiled, and has the smoothness of early maturity, his face rounded by a lifetime of good nourishment. No worry lines around the eyes or mouth. He moves easily, sure of his place in the community. All possible because of his wealth: money, land and possessions. There's more. He's a ruler, a fully paid-up member of the establishment.

His confidence though is superficial. Below the pampered surface he's unsure of himself, although it's something well hidden until now. As he approaches the crowd, ordinary folk recognise him, step aside respectfully, and let him pass. He hardly notices and certainly doesn't acknowledge. It's his due. He holds his robe close – you can never tell whom you might touch, or who might touch you in the throng. So, he reaches the crowd's edge and stands, until he sees Jesus. There's something about Jesus he recognises. It's hard to define, but he notes the authority, the purity and, more surprisingly, the welcome he gives to all who approach him. This is the man, the teacher everyone is talking about.

The aristocrat seems thoughtful. His eyes move from Jesus to the onlookers, and back again. He takes a deep breath and let's it out slowly as he makes up his mind. Then he says to himself, "I don't care what people think, I'm going to ask him." A sudden decision. He purses his lips, looks around for a last glance at all the people, and moves. He quickens his step and pushes through the crowd, all thought of keeping himself apart forgotten. He's committed.

He stands in front of Jesus. No sideways approach for him. He speaks quietly but with an uncharacteristic hesitation. Jesus responds with a smile. They talk for a few minutes; only those closest to them hear the words. Then Jesus puts his hand on the man's arm with a look of love that slowly turns to sadness. At the same time the young man's smile freezes. He looks puzzled, disappointed. He hesitates, shrugs and tries to respond but finds no more words. Just a murmured apology as he turns away. He moves unseeing, no longer confident, head down, shoulders drooping. Jesus watches him until he's hidden by the crowd. He shakes his head slowly, regretfully, and turns to his disciples with a sigh.

A certain ruler asked him," Good teacher, what must I do to inherit eternal life?" "Why do you call me good? "Jesus answered. "No-one is good – except God alone."

Luke 18:18

We need two Gospels to describe the man, even though we end up with just three words. Matthew says he was a young man. Luke writes that he was a ruler, and wealthy (Mark too). So he comes into our world as the rich young ruler. That's the heading given to the story in all three Gospels, although the headings and verse numbers in our Bibles were added many centuries after they were written, to make it easier to find a particular event. Today we call it sub-editing.

Young, rich, healthy, and from Israel's top-drawer society. We've moved from Capernaum to a location we can't identify, and it's not clear what he ruled. He was probably a member of a synagogue committee, a younger version of Jairus. He's heard a lot about Jesus, both for and against. By this time, Jesus was becoming an irritant to those in authority, but this man was looking beyond the criticism he'd heard, and had begun to feel that there was something deep, real and direct in Jesus' teaching. As he stands listening on the edge of the gathering, he realises that Jesus is special. He screws up his courage and goes to him.

It would take courage to go to Jesus and admit publicly by his question that he felt the need for a deeper spirituality than his position and lifestyle had given him. His question is sincere. Most 'rulers' asked trick questions, designed to embarrass Jesus, or to provoke an answer that would land him in trouble with the authorities. That's not the young man's intention. He truly wants to understand. He feels there's something missing from his own life and wants to fill the gap. Behind the self-confidence, his head is full of questions. Yes, he keeps the commandments meticulously, but it's lifeless. He yearns for something more.

"Good teacher," he begins, addressing Jesus. Jesus takes up the word *good*. The word can be used in many ways. My copy of the *Oxford English Dictionary* takes more than a full page of small print to describe its many uses. The writer, G.K. Chesterton, once said that "if a man shot his mother-in-law at 500 yards, he could be described as a good shot, but not necessarily as a good man."

I doubt if the young man had actually given much thought to the word; it just seemed the most appropriate and polite form of address, with maybe a hint of flattery. Jesus doesn't let it pass. He points the young man's attention, and that of the onlookers, away from himself and towards God, the source of all goodness. That's where Jesus' goodness came from: and the young man's too, if he had any. There's a humility at the heart of Jesus, which the young man might well copy, a grace and gift from God.

Lord, I know how he was feeling,
the rich young man.
Let me explain,
although I realise you already know.
Can't say I'm rich,
although the starving millions in the world today
would say I am,
and certainly not young,
which leaves me – still a man.
But yet I know just how he felt.

It was the heartache, Lord.
The feeling deep inside
that said however hard he tried
he'd missed the core of it.
He'd tried, God knew.
You knew.
Piled on the rules.
Heaped them in suffocating drifts,
then gloried in their weight.
And thought himself
a cut above the rest in doing it.
Yet in the quiet moments,
those sleepless hours in the night,
when he, half waking,
stares into the darkness,
and wonders what he has to do
to hear your voice
and feel your presence close.

I know that feeling too,
and thank you for it, Lord,
because it comes from you,
your spirit
working wonders from within,
drawing me on,
my loneliness the instrument
that pulls me ever nearer to its source.

And when, the struggle laid aside,
I find my resting place in you,
I wonder why the struggle took so long.
Your arms so gentle yet so strong,
welcome me in
and lovingly remind me
you were there beside me
all the time.

"All these I have kept since I was a boy," he said.

Luke 18:21

"What must I do to inherit eternal life?" A good question, but the young man's got it the wrong way round. I notice two words: *do* and *inherit*. Here's a man from a wealthy family; brought up in privilege and expecting to inherit the family jewels. And everything else. He hasn't earned it all, he's simply been born on the right side of the railway tracks, or whatever the equivalent was in Jesus' day. He's obeyed family traditions, behaved well, and married the right sort of girl. And, in due course, the family fortune will be his. He's kept the rules, but rules kept meticulously can be cold and loveless. It had been, was still, hard work, and he thought perhaps he'd earned some reward.

But there's a seed germinating uncomfortably in the border of his mind that suggests to him that this isn't enough. In spite of all his efforts at rule-keeping since he became a man, below the surface he still feels incomplete, unfulfilled. Yet he can only fashion his question in terms of what he must *do*. He assumes that if he can take on board a few more rules from Jesus, his future will be secure, and eternal life will be assured. "What must I do?" he asks.

Jesus accepts his sincerity, and welcomes the question. He refers him to the commandments, concentrating on those that cover human relationships; Matthew's account adds one more, about loving your neighbour. The man answers confidently, although I suspect he was not being totally honest, speaking more to impress Jesus and the folk around them. He's describing perfection, something belonging only to God. Yet Jesus sees his eagerness, his desire for a deeper experience of God, even though his question is the wrong way round. Now, can he redirect his energy and take just one step of faith to gain what he's missing? A step that would lead to a lifetime of total and joyful commitment and a freedom he'd never known.

Just one more step, Lord,
a little step,
and yet the biggest step
that he could ever take.
And me.

I've cleared, I think,
the basic problem of assuming
I could earn
a complimentary ticket to a seat –
not necessarily the best,
a back-row view would suit me well –
within your kingdom.

I've learned, Lord, too,
that in those precious moments
when the truth takes over,
uncomfortable as it is,
that though it is the way
the world we live in works,
it isn't so in yours.

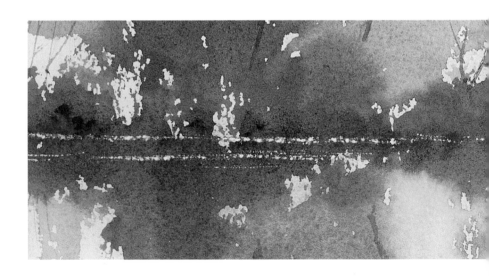

Yours works through love
and in love's kingdom all the seats are free,
no pillars in the way,
the view complete.

The ticket price?
Easiest – and hardest – of them all.
Just open up my life without conditions
and your kingdom's door
will open wide.
Is open wide already.
So simple and so hard to do.
To gather up my strength
and leap into your love.
A love that wraps me safe,
not in the soft and comforting
hot-chocolate-kind of love,
but love's espresso,
strong, dark and challenging,
that wakes me up
to think and work for you.

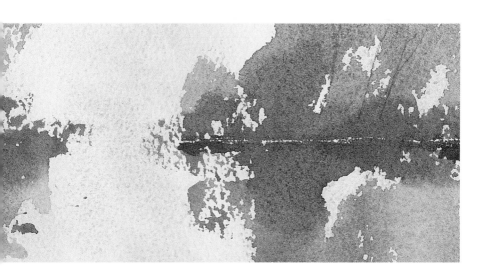

Through the Trees

From your side – love unlimited.
From mine – I know, I know,
it's simply opening up my life to yours.

Watercolour

Jesus looked at him and loved him.

Mark 10:21

Jesus loves him. Loves him for his dedicated attempt to be 'good', even though it was leading him the wrong way up a one-way street. He loves him for his sincerity and because the young man recognises his need. And because he has the nerve to come to Jesus publicly and admit it. Jesus loves him, and yearns that he may find the courage to take one step more into the freedom he offers. Didn't Jesus love everyone? Yes, certainly, in the sense of sharing their needs and wanting them to become what God created them to be, but there's a feeling of something more here. Why else would Mark make such a point of it in recounting the story? Jesus must have seen some special quality in this young man, some possibility waiting to be released. Although, again, I believe this is the way Jesus looks at each of us, believes in each of us.

How Jesus' heart longed for him. How ready to welcome and accept him. Yet that same love is unwilling, even unable, to exert pressure on him, to violate his personal space. He is welcomed with love, and love will follow him. The choice would be his. At this moment, the man couldn't take the leap of faith Jesus was asking for, but I suspect that the door to eternal life would remain open for him. His hunger for God, for new life, would always be there, lurking in the corners of his heart. And God is forgiving. His arms still open, the door still ajar, for whenever the young man can break with his past. With time, as the Holy Spirit continues to nibble away at his hesitation, he will find the courage to break through to new life. Jesus offered him the chance to jump from fear to freedom. Underneath painstaking rule-keeping lurks the fear of failure. One mistake and the whole structure crumbles. But in Jesus, rules give place to freedom, where the only rule is love and mistakes forgiven.

Eternal life was nothing he could earn or buy, not even with a Platinum Visa credit card. It asks for one great leap of faith. A leap into a darkness that becomes light as you leap, jumping from the known and comfortable into a new life of adventure, where the only certainty is the presence and encouragement of Jesus, and the sure knowledge that he will walk with you on the path. It's significant that this story comes straight after that of Jesus welcoming little children and saying that those who covet the kingdom must enter like them. In John's Gospel there's another 'ruler', a Pharisee named Nicodemus. He comes to Jesus secretly at night, and is told he must be born again to enter the community of God. (John 3:3) And in rebirth we bond with Jesus as a new-born child bonds with its mother. Rebirth and resurrection are twins. Being born again, whether a dramatic, time-and-date event or a slow process of grafting into faith, is followed by a lifetime's walk with Christ. No wonder the young man thinks twice, but what an opportunity he misses, to share in the mystery and joy of resurrection. In this new life, says Margaret Silf, what Jesus "is asking of him and of us, however, is not so much that we learn to do exactly what he does, but that we seek to be more like who he is."*

* Quiet Spaces – The Journey, *Bible Reading Fellowship 2005*

Lord, sometimes I think you offer
too much freedom.
A little pressure here and there,
a push, a nudge,
even a well-timed elbow,
sharp in the ribs of my reluctance,
might steer me sheepishly –
you talked of sheep and shepherds, Lord,
not wanting even one to go astray –
into the pen.
But I'll admit that sheep
can turn and run the other way,
and sheepdog rules that bark
and threaten me
may never bring me, panting,
into your kingdom.

From your side – love unlimited.
From mine – I know, I know,
it's simply opening up my life to yours.
Or not so simply.
I like to make my own decisions,
and yet I'm asking you
to use a little pressure –
not very logical I recognise –
to draw me in.

There is, I grant,
an element of pride
in my approach to you.
I like to think
that somehow, still,
I can impress occasionally
with appropriate behaviour.
But, in the depths of what I call –
it must give you a smile at times –
my conscience,
your patient voice comes, yet again,
so quietly
but never quite drowned out,
offering me the gift of love.

And, knowing that,
when I am on my own
and no-one's looking except you,
I am a little prone to shouting,
Hallelujah!

"You still lack one thing. Sell everything you have and give to the poor, and you will have treasure in heaven. Then come, follow me." When he heard this, he became very sad, because he was a man of very great wealth.

Luke 18:22-23

"You lack one thing," said Jesus. Faith isn't about rules, it's about relationships. If you love God, it will show in love for your neighbour in practical ways. Maybe his family wealth had been gained by the labour and exploitation of the poor, and in his wisdom, Jesus is suggesting that there needs to be a balance. A message for today. Riches may not be intrinsically wrong, but we are called to use them and share them at least with justice, better with compassion.

It's good news and bad news for the eager young man. Couldn't Jesus have dealt with him more gently? Did he have to hit him quite so hard with the demand to give up everything that seemed to make his life good? If Jesus had been a little softer in his reply, might not the young man have stepped forward and followed? Jesus, it says, looked at him and loved him. Couldn't that love have been expressed in a more persuasive way? Apparently not. The man has been fully committed to his lifestyle of rules; if he truly wants to change, it must be equally radical.

Jesus sees a man brought up in comfort, never worrying about the next meal, and never having to struggle for work or status. Yet he recognises the sincerity and his strong commitment to living well. It can't have been easy obeying so carefully the commandments on which he'd based his life. Maybe there was a hint of pride in claiming that he had kept them all, but that's what he believed. It must have taken years of self-control and denial, but he's still aware of the empty space in his life. It was this unnamed yearning that brought him and his question to Jesus.

The man's at crisis point. He hesitates, but the challenge is too much. Deeply disappointed he shakes his head, sighs, and turns away. At least he was honest. He could have said that he'd go home and think about it or, as some of us say when we're faced with something we don't like, "I'll go home and pray about it," – although I wonder if we always do? The young man had so wanted an answer, but couldn't face one so demanding. As it was, I imagine him looking at the disciples around Jesus – fishermen, an ex-tax collector, and others, carrying their possessions in cloth bundles on their shoulders – not the sort of companions he was used to. Jesus was asking for everything.

The young man's grip on his wealth, or rather his wealth's grip on him, was too strong to break through. Jesus' demand was tough love, as Americans say. It's so easy to weaken the claims of faith and ask for less, in the hope that it will draw people in. Maybe that sometimes works but it can lead to disillusion, as folk learn from life that faith can be demanding and the way stony.

You let him walk away, Lord.
That's something I find hard to understand.
You loved him, so it's said
and yet you let him go.
If I had loved like that –
forgive me, Lord,
I'd never claim
a tiny fraction of the love you show –
I would have given him another chance.
I'd follow, call, ask him to wait and listen.
Perhaps a longer conversation,
explaining what you'd meant,
might just have tipped the scales.
But you stood still and let him go.
Just that one opportunity,
that's all he had,
and in that moment of decision
he turned around and walked away.

The problem is your love gives freedom.
We're free to choose our path,
to make our own decisions,
so even though you loved
and wanted him to follow
he, and he alone,
could make the choice.
And that was that.

But then I wonder –
you are the living, loving image of your father
and I can't believe you'd let him go forever.
I'm sure that as he walked away
your love, your prayers,
your very self went with him,
willing him to open up his heart
to what you'd said.
Continuing to work your will in him
as in so many others.

In me, Lord, too.
I've tried at times to walk away,
choose my own path,
but when I've reached its end
I've found you waiting there for me.
Your welcome just as warm
your smile as sure,
your love just as forgiving.
It's all I need.
I'll let it rest at that.

...your love, your prayers,
your very self went with him,
willing him to open up his heart
to what you'd said.

Tranquil Trees

Watercolour

Jesus looked at him and said, "How hard it is for the rich to enter the kingdom of God! Indeed, it is easier for a camel to go through the eye of a needle than for a rich man to enter the kingdom of God." Those who heard this asked, "Who then can be saved?" Jesus replied, "What is impossible with men is possible with God."

Luke 18:24-27

If all things are possible with God, I'd love to watch that camel squeezing through the eye of a needle. I can see the pained expression in the camel's eye, and the disdainful curl of its lip. And as for his hump? But before I go further down that path let's get back to the question.

The young man turns away. He's dissatisfied with his life, still feels a hunger for something he can't express, but he can't make that commitment. He's not alone. The 4th Century Saint Augustine, prayed, "Lord, make me pure, but not yet." An attitude echoed down the ages and felt by many today. The pull of the known, the familiar and comfortable, is too great.

Jesus' love and sadness follow the young man. So much effort, so much promise, such great possibilities in him. If only. "How hard it is," says Jesus, "for the rich to enter the kingdom of God." Years ago, Pope John Paul visited the United Kingdom. My wife, Barbara, and I were fortunate to be given tickets for a special service in which he took part in Canterbury Cathedral. Security was tight. As we stood in line waiting to be admitted, several Anglican bishops stood in front of us. One couldn't find his invitation card and we were all held up. I spoke to a bishop next to me. I said, "I wonder if it will be like this at the Pearly Gates? All of us held up by a bishop who's lost his admission card?" The bishop laughed, and we moved on. I doubt if the Pharisees would have smiled.

Jesus doesn't say it's impossible, just hard. No-one is excluded automatically. Everyone, rich or poor, has the chance to share in the life God offers. Then with a sudden shift of mood – and possibly noticing a string of camels passing along the road behind the crowd – Jesus tries to lighten the atmosphere. The disciples and crowd are surprised. They thought riches were a sign of God's blessing, just as illness and poverty were a judgement. If those who had been blessed with wealth by God, and who could buy themselves into anything, would find it hard to enter the kingdom, then who could share in it?

Implicit in Jesus' words is a warning not to judge others. Jesus had already broken through the rules by welcoming the faith of a Roman centurion, and healing a woman thrown out by her community. He'd told the gathering that there'd be many like the centurion whom God would accept for their faith before many of the 'chosen'. When my prejudices are activated, I find it easy to decide who's going to be part of the kingdom and, to be honest, even easier to decide who'll be left outside. "It's not up to you to judge," Jesus warned them. A judgemental attitude judges those who judge. I think of some church groups who transform the wide, forgiving love of God into a short checklist of behaviour, which immediately identifies and separates the saved and, neatly but cruelly, the unsaved. An attitude more about control and power than it is about forgiveness and love. I don't think Jesus would have recognised the process. Someone said that God doesn't see us as bad or good. He sees us as lost or found, and never abandons the lost.

The disciples are shocked. Peter is the first to react. He and the others still see life in traditional terms. "We've left everything to follow you; our fishing boats, our livelihoods and families..." Implying the question, "Does that mean we're in or out?" In Jesus' reply, it's not the act of renouncing possessions that's required, but the reordering of priorities. All who put God's rule first are welcomed. It's the loving commitment to follow Jesus that counts, and that's what the rich young man couldn't bring himself to give. But if faith is weak, don't give up. If we haven't the courage to surrender all now, follow anyway. He walks with us, and supplies the courage and the faith to keep going.

It's not just a promise for the future. Those who open their lives to God's rule will be blessed 'in this age'. (Luke 18:30) Not with wealth or comfort, a mistaken assumption some make even today, but with a closer experience of the presence of Jesus. It begins here and now for all who say 'Yes'. In following him, our lives are deepened, our horizons widened. New life breaks through, in ways not always easy to recognise, and sometimes bringing pressures and consequences we'd rather not have, but this new life is the presence of Jesus himself. What more can anyone ask? And what more can anyone want?

Lord, I too have walked away,
not once but many times,
when your demands have seemed –
forgive me yet again –
unreasonable.
Asking for all I am and all I have,
and in exchange for what?
An uncertain future.
I've looked and thought,
shaken my head and turned away.
But I have learnt the hard way, Lord,
sometimes the only way,
that you're not shaken off so easily.

That when I've turned around,
gone my own way,
there's still a thread
that draws me back to you.
A gentle hand,
a murmuring voice,
so full of love
that I am captivated once again.

And when I'm at my most rebellious,
your voice is at its best,
so patient and persistent.
All I can do is wonder and return,
knowing there is no way
that I can break so light a chain.

And when we're back together
you and me,
I realise with joy
we never were apart.
Because wherever I may go,
we walk each step together.
Your love too gracious
and forgiving to give up.
And that uncertain future
I was so frightened of
is the one thing
that is certain in this world.

Lord, thank you.

Safe Harbour

O Lord our God, grant us grace to desire you

with our whole heart;

that so desiring, we may seek,

and seeking find you;

and so finding you, may love you;

and loving you,

may hate those sins

from which you have redeemed us.

Anselm, Archbishop of Canterbury, 11th Century AD

Watercolour

Eddie and Barbara Askew joined The Leprosy Mission in 1950. After 15 years serving in India, they transferred to London where Eddie became International Director of the Mission's worldwide operations. Eddie retired in 1987 and was then able to devote more time to his love of writing and painting. When he died in 2007, he had written 17 bestselling Christian books. We will always be grateful to him for his dedication and leadership and we will never forget his compassion, creativity and great sense of humour.

OTHER BOOKS WRITTEN AND ILLUSTRATED BY EDDIE ASKEW

A SILENCE AND A SHOUTING
Eddie's first compilation of 32 Bible readings, prayers and meditations.

DISGUISES OF LOVE
Eddie explores the disguises of love revealed through the pain and suffering of Christ.

MANY VOICES ONE VOICE
31 prayers and meditations that help us to listen out for God's voice amidst the daily clamour of life.

NO STRANGE LAND
'There is no strange land to God. His love, compassion and healing are at work wherever we are.'

FACING THE STORM
A book that encourages us to hang on to our faith while we wait for the storm to pass.

BREAKING THE RULES
When Jesus broke the rules of Jewish society, he demonstrated that the essence of life is not in law but in loving.

CROSS PURPOSES
Eddie shows us that 'The purpose of Jesus' cross is to cancel out the cross purposes of the world.'

SLOWER THAN BUTTERFLIES
Life is fast these days; Eddie invites us to step aside for a few moments each day and pause for thought.

MUSIC ON THE WIND
Eddie encourages us to hear the music of God's love as he takes us through the life of David.

EDGE OF DAYLIGHT
Eddie's fascinating memoirs of his life with TLM, notably his 15 years as a missionary in India and his later travels across the world as TLM's International Director.

TALKING WITH HEDGEHOGS
35 *Thoughts for the Day* that encourage us to think about how we influence our own lives and those of the people around us.

UNEXPECTED JOURNEYS
Here, Eddie gives his uniquely imaginative interpretation of five familiar Bible stories, exploring the significance of the journey each character makes. Beautiful illustrations, plus a guide to using his paintings in meditation.

LOVE IS A WILD BIRD
'Love is a wild bird... Give it the freedom to fly and, if it returns, it's truly yours.' One of many inspiring thoughts in this splendid collection.

ENCOUNTERS
Five characters encounter Jesus face-to-face and their lives are wonderfully transformed.

CHASING THE LEAVES
Stories and anecdotes that will make you smile, wonder or simply pause for thought.

ALL OF THESE BOOKS CAN BE BOUGHT FROM TLM TRADING LIMITED
Telephone 0845 166 2253 or shop online at www.tlmtrading.com